NEPATIZED!

NEPATIZED!

Behind the People and Controversies that Define Us

Author of *Thumbing Through Thoreau: A Book of Quotations by Henry David Thoreau*

KENNY LUCK

AVENTURA
PRESS

ISBN-13:
978-1-936936-00-7

Published by
Avventura Press

www.avventurapress.com

1ˢᵗ printing April 2011
Printed in the United States of America

DEDICATION

In 1676, the scientist Sir Isaac Newtown wrote in a letter, "If I have seen further it is only by standing on the shoulder of giants." Newton's wonderful observation acknowledges the people and knowledge that had come before him, and I would like to take a moment to do the same.

I wrote this book, inspired by the intellectual giants—past and present—who have dedicated their lives the Enlightenment values, reason, and the search for truth. The work of these brilliant men has helped shape thought and inquiry throughout the centuries, and their importance shall not be overlooked. Thank you for your inspiration.

Socrates, Henry David Thoreau, Charles Darwin, David Hume, Christopher Hitchens, Franz Kafka, Thomas Jefferson, James Madison, Richard Dawkins, John Paul Sartre, Richard Hofstadter, Michael Shermer, Ralph Waldo Emerson, and James Randi.

～

I would also like to thank my friends and acquaintances, for their unlimited kindness, and for their encouragement over the years.

My Mom and family, Ann Bush, Kathleen Munley, Barbra Hoffman, Michael Foley, Phil Yurkon, Michael Jozaitis, Ryan Ward, Jessica Jellen, Mark Bakos, Jack Bobinshot, Dave Evans, Patrick Tindana, Mike Bennett, Justin Vacula, Jo-Ann Wald, The Staff at Borders in Dickson City, PA, Darcy and Jim Ford, Julia Glukoy, Mike Tomalis, John Nadrotowicz, Jenny Tigue, my students, and Avventura Press.

CONTENTS

INTRODUCTION

Driving southbound on Interstate 81 one cold afternoon in February, 2008, I realized that my CD player had stopped working.

"What's the problem *now*?" I thought.

A recent college graduate, and the owner of a dilapidated '92 Toyota Camry, I had no money and no real job prospects. I had become used to things breaking on my car, so a crippled CD player was just one more thing to bear. For months, I had been working at a refrigerated food warehouse in Pittston—organizing boxes and making deliveries—and could not afford to get my stereo fixed. Living on a mere $200 a week, I had to commute to and from work without the company of my favorite music.

But soon I began scanning the radio, which had survived, in an attempt to find something that would relieve the silence and soften the humming of the engine. I always enjoyed the edifying stories featured on National Public Radio (NPR), but I wasn't always in the mood for intellectual banter. But then, one day, I found something else: *WILK*.

WILK—the megaphone for right-wing discontent in the region—operates under the absurd premise that it accurately represents the mindset of Northeastern Pennsylvania when, in fact, it represents the viewpoint of nothing but conservatism and cantankerous, cynical old men who primarily compose its listenership. Perverse and opinionated, the station spreads controversies, and sometimes fabricates them, through baseless gossip and faux "news" reporting. Within a few weeks, I had become consumed by the station's lack of objective reporting and its self-parodying style. I was hooked, and soon began to analyze everything.

Thus began my fascination with local current events. Having spent time traveling around the United States during my undergraduate years, pursing a Kerouacian "beatitude," and visiting places like New Orleans, LA, just after Hurricane Katrina; the Badlands of South Dakota; the urban landscape of Los Angeles, CA; and the deserts of the American Southwest—I had always been more focused on national and global issues. But a few years later, after college, I began to think about the local and the immediate.

As a resident of Wilkes-Barre, PA, in Luzerne County, I have had a front row seat to the nonsensical corruption which has been dominating the news. A voracious reader and thinker, I began to see these issues, not as a series isolated events, but as cohesive ethos manifesting itself throughout the region in multiple ways. Moreover, if one accepts the premise that actions are a reflection of beliefs, than the thinking of Northeastern Pennsylvania is just as corrupt as the public officials it continually votes into office.

~

Using qualitative research methods as well as various journalistic approaches to support my assertions, I cited primary source documents, consulted news reports, attended events, and—most importantly—conducted interviews. In addition, *The Associated Press Stylebook* was a valuable asset to my research. With almost 300 footnotes, a nine page bibliography, and 30 interviews, this short book is well-documented, well-researched, and well-supported.

By "triangulating" sources, I hope to get the clearest, most reliable information available and apply it to my thesis: The social and political culture of Northeastern Pennsylvania is based primarily on sensationalist news stories, and has been reduced to a spectacle of unequivocal idiocy, unseen at any time in the past. Whether it was Bishop Martino raging against homosexuals and secular values in 2008, or the corrupt and careless actions of Cabot Oil and Gas in 2010, the region has been under siege by hucksters, fundamentalists, and frauds.

But not everyone fits this description. I learned a great deal from the subjects I interviewed, and admire their courage. Dawn Winarski and Michael Milz, for instance, had to endure an onslaught of attacks from church authorities simply because they stood up for their beliefs. More particularly, Milz received death threats because he believed that diocese employees should have union representation. Justin Vacula, the college student who contacted the American Civil Liberties Union (ACLU) over Luzerne County's Christmas Display in late 2009, was bitterly attacked and denounced by so-called "devout" individuals. Finally, Sarah Gaia, who requested that her real name not be used, fought tirelessly against the oil and gas companies, only to be shunned and ignored, but her fight continues.

It is through the actions of these individuals, and others, which remind me that hope is not lost. As I sat conversing with my subjects, I heard stories that were too important to shun or ignore. I learned that there were real lives behind the local headlines, people who were suffering from the scandals, controversies, and corruption—who had a lot at stake and much to lose, who were at the center of some of the most pivotal current events of our time, and did not falter.

～

This book is not a dry retelling of events; it is the *interpretation* of events by one young man. My intent is this:

To weave together eight seemingly unrelated people and events into a coherent narrative. This narrative—the story of Northeastern Pennsylvania in recent years—demonstrates who and what has defined the region.

Of course, many are outraged by the revelations of corruption and scandal in Luzerne and Lackawanna County. The sinister acts of greed are, simply put, inexcusable. But I am interested in a more central question: How do these crimes change a region's self-image and overall outlook? With the elder generations dying, and the new influx of immigrants replacing them, Northeastern Pennsylvania is facing an identity crisis. All of this, coupled by crumbing county and local governments, provokes postulation and reflection. But instead of asking ontological questions about the nature of who we are, and who we want to be, many in the region have become NEPATIZED. We need to begin having a conversation which enables a discourse of reason—not, as the state of current affairs stands, a discourse of distraction.

Consider Lou Barletta. Barletta is a one-issue politician who uses his notoriety for political gain. Barletta is known best for his Hazelton anti-immigration ordinance enacted in 2006, while he was mayor. But I do not believe in the sincerity of his cause although, sadly, many do. In March 2010, while attending *The Weekender's* annual "Reader's Choice" Award Ceremony at Mohegan Sun Casino, I crossed paths with the savvy politician. Dressed elegantly and nursing a drink at the bar, Barletta was surrounded by hordes of sycophantic admirers. The Hazelton Mayor was awarded "Best Politician" by *Weekender* voters, and I thought that could not be more appropriate. He is undoubtedly a master politician, but his merits as a public servant are questionable. I left the V.I.P. event wondering if I could get an interview with him: He never returned any of my phone calls.

⁓

There is nothing sexy or glamorous about the craft of writing. The image of the lone intellectual, slaving over his or her work is portrayed as a noble pursuit—and it is. But crafting words and sentences is much more than this old, clichéd image. This particular book was born out of long afternoons in coffee shops, hot cups of tea, and the determination to compose a cogent and consistent argument based on facts, observations, and evidence about the world around me.

The tedious editing of interview transcripts, reading long documents, and revising multiple drafts are the tools of writing journalistic prose. I applied these methods and produced the bulk of this book between March and May 2010, just as I was finishing my graduate course work and my first book, *Thumbing Through Thoreau: A Book of Quotations by Henry David Thoreau* (Tribute Books, 2010).

The danger with writing about current events is, of course, that their status as "current" does not last long: the content quickly becomes outmoded, and in an age of infotainment, each news story has a lifespan about that of a gnat fly. Nevertheless, the stories and events contained in this short book are emblematic of Northeastern Pennsylvania *as it is*. In other words, this book is a snapshot in time. There is a larger truth hidden within the ephemera of daily events, and *NEPATIZED!* is my best attempt to make sense of the chaos which has engulfed our community.

—*Kenny Luck*
December 2010

one

The Real Barletta

"He could have dealt with illegal immigration by enforcing other laws. He didn't have to do this. After all the problems it caused after that, Hazelton really sounded like a very bigoted city across the nation. We're rednecks around here, so people loved it."

—Dee Deakos, *Hazleton Resident and 2007 Mayoral Candidate*

Lou Barletta entered into wide public discourse when, as mayor, the City of Hazelton enacted an ordinance that classified certain immigrants (usually those who came from Latin America) as "illegal," made English the "official language" of the city, and punished landlords and employers for conducting any business with alleged "alien" residents.[1] Barletta was elected

---

1   American Civil Liberties Union of Pennsylvania, "Hazelton Residents Sue to Halt Harsh Anti-Immigration Law," *ACLU of Pennsylvania,* 15 August 2006 <http://www.aclupa.org/pressroom/hazletonresidentssuetohalt.htm>

Mayor of Hazelton in 2000, and his tenure lasted roughly a decade. Apart from his anti-immigrant endeavors in recent years, this nativistic politician has made attempts to claim the 11th District Congressional seat from long-time Democrat Paul Kanjorski in 2002 and 2008, and lost on both occasions. But in November 2010, Barletta finally ended Paul Kanjorski's 13-term congressional career.

Blogger Dan Cheek, who operates the blog StopLouBarletta.com, believes that Barletta has used illegal immigration as a wedge issue to divert the public's attention away from his dubious fiscal policies. "He really wasn't speaking to any of the issues that every other politician had to be accountable for," Cheek said, while discussing Barletta's 2008 congressional campaign. "He seemed to get a pass by screaming about illegal immigration over and over. His strategy seems to be, as it always is, to throw up the illegal immigration smokescreen."[2]

Interestingly, Cheek is a long-time Republican, but does not think Barletta is representative of the party. Speaking prior to the November 2010 elections, Cheek did not hide is contempt for Barletta. "The Republican Party continues to drop him off as a candidate," he said. "But the fact that he is going to be the only representative for the Republican Party is a sad day for them."[3]

Cheek's blog has been instrumental in raising awareness of the former mayor. Created in April 2008, the website is a resource for documents, information, and opinions about Barletta. "All the facts that I have are all linked to things that have appeared in the *Scranton-Times*, *The Standard Speaker* and *The Citizens Voice*," he explained. "If Bar-

---

2   Dan Cheek, interview by Kenny Luck, 9 April 2010.
3   Ibid.

letta wants to respond to anything on the website, I've offered to post his response unedited, without commentary, and he's never taken me up on it. I've gotten a lot of support from the city of Hazelton," he said. "They've been very supportive of the blog and contacted me, thanking me because there is no other outlet for them to voice any kind of opposition to Barletta. There is a lot of pent up opposition to Barletta in his city."[4]

After gaining the blessings of the Republican Party, Barletta focused on the November 2010 elections in his third attempt to go to Washington. "He has aims for higher office. I don't know how serious even he is about accomplishing this," Cheek commented before the 2010 midterms. "If you look at what he has done in the previous election, he really didn't perform that well."

But Barletta, 52, performed well in 2010—winning 55 percent of the vote—and ended Kanjorski's 26 years in office, also becoming the first Republican to win the 11th District in decades.[5] Professor Terry Madonna, who directs the Franklin and Marshall College Poll, speaking months before the general election, believed that Barletta would put up a competitive race. "In this year, in a much more favorable Republican environment, with Republican voters more likely to vote than Democratic voters... I think that is going to be a close race and competitive race," Madonna said, while in an interview. With a combined 12,700 television attack ads from both Barletta and Kanjorski during the campaign, the mudslinging between the candidates

4   Ibid.
5   Andrew Staub and Mia Light, "Kanjorski Falls," *The Citizen's Voice* 3 November 2010.

continued unmitigated for months.[6] In the end, however, Barletta was able to out-smear Kanjorski.

Xenophobic Tendencies

In August 2006, the Hazelton City Council passed the Illegal Immigration Relief Act. The ordinance was questionable, and its constitutionality was immediately challenged. The legislation was an attempt to halt the spread of immigration which, as Barletta attempted to argue, was the cause of a recent crime surge, over-crowded schools, and strained social-services in Hazelton.[7] The mayor pointed out that "a high-profile murder, the discharge of a gun at a crowded city playground, and drug busts,"[8] were enough evidence to rationalize his xenophobic actions toward ethnic minorities. Adopting a bullet-proof vest as part of his wardrobe, Barletta vowed to make Hazelton one of the "toughest places in the United States" for illegal immigrants.[9] He even invented his own slogan: "You Are Not Welcome."

But not everyone believes in Barletta's rationale. Hazelton resident Dee Deakos, who attempted to unseat Barletta in the 2007 Hazelton mayoral election, questions his motivation. "People were upset because a group of Hispanics started moving in," she said. "But they weren't all illegal. If they are from Puerto Rico, they're legal. They're Americans."[10]

Deakos maintains that the illegal issue began when

6   Charles Schillinger and Steve McConnell, "For Lou Barletta, Third Time's a Charm," *The Times-Tribune*, 3 November 2010.
7   Amy Worden, "U.S. House Entices Hazelton Mayor," *The Philadelphia Inquirer*, 8 February 2008.
8   <www.smalltowndefenders.com>
9   Julia Preston, "Judge Voids Ordinance on Illegal Immigrants," *The New York Times*, 7 July 2007.
10   Dee Deakos, interview by Kenny Luck, 5 May 2010.

"one man was shot by two illegals, and Barletta decided this was the time to take a stand."[11] Moreover, Deakos points out that, quite arbitrarily, "all the previous murders which were against Hispanics, he ignored. They were gang related, and Barletta didn't care about them." Cheek, like Deakos, believes that Barletta's reduction of the police force as mayor is what contributed to the crime wave—not illegal immigrants. "His next act was to cut the Hazelton police force in half because of budget issues," he recalled. "As a result, crime went up and that's when he started spewing about this illegal immigration crime wave. This was one of the issues that came up when he was defending this in court, and they actually asked him for numbers. The crime data that he released was less than one percent of all crimes committed in Hazelton over the span of five years were actually attributed to undocumented aliens. The rest were all locals."[12]

The attention surrounding the controversial ordinance landed Barletta in the national spotlight, making him the darling of many "America First" nativists with radical ideological leanings. "That all started because someone got shot, and the person who shot him were illegals," Deakos said. "Why didn't immigration deport them then and there? There is a federal law saying that if you commit a certain type of crime, which they did, they get deported. Rather

---

11 Ibid.
12 Kris Kobach, a Professor of Law at the University of Missouri-Kansas City, argues that crimes committed by illegal aliens were much higher. Kobach argues that "Drug crimes increased, with illegal aliens representing 30 percent of those arrested." However, Kobach fails to cite where he obtained this statistic. His claim is challenged by David F. Prenatt, who in a July 2006 article entitled, "Illegal Immigration and Crime in Hazelton, Pennsylvania," explains in detail the particulars of Hazelton's crime statistics.
<http://www.smalltowndefenders.com/node/229>
<http://blog.netesq.com/2006/07/illegal-immigration-and-crime-in.html>

than do something that he did, just quietly deport them."[13] These facts did nothing to deter Barletta's popularity. Many, such as former CNN News Commentator Lou Dobbs, vehemently supported the mayor. But most noteworthy was David Duke, a former Grand Wizard of the Ku Klux Klan. Duke is a well-known white supremacist and racist who, for a short time (1989 to 1992), was a Republican member of the House of Representatives from the state of Louisiana.[14] On his website, Duke touted that he "has dedicated his life to the freedom and heritage of European American peoples," and describes himself as a man of "both intellect and courage."

When Barletta announced his bid for Congress in early 2008, Duke enthusiastically endorsed the Hazelton Mayor. "Getting tough patriots like Lou Barletta elected," Duke

MEMORABLE MOMENTS

During the 2008 election between Republican Lou Barletta and Democrat Paul Kanjorski, an ad sponsored by a Political Action Committee in Washington D.C. called "Team America," which favored Barletta, used subtle music and images to suggest that Kanjorski was somehow an advocate of illegal immigration.

---

13   Dee Deakos, interview by Kenny Luck, 5 May 2010.
14   <http://en.wikipedia.org/wiki/David_Duke>

wrote, "is absolutely key to staving off four years of sustained attack on our European American interests."[15] Duke wrote that his organization, European Americans United, is not affiliated with Barletta and that "he would probably disagree with many of our positions," but added: "We like him and hope he wins."[16]

Barletta never addressed the Duke endorsement. "Barletta never actually came out and distanced himself from that. He said: 'I have no control over who endorses me.' From my perspective," Cheek continued, "if a former leader of the Ku Klux Klan is coming out and endorsing you, you would think that he would come out adamantly against that. He never did, and I thought that that spoke volumes about him."[17]

A Linguistic Mandate

The Official English Language Ordinance states that: "The City Council, Mayor, and Officials of the City of Hazleton shall take all steps necessary to insure the role of English as the common language of the city...." What is more, the ordinance added: "In addition to any other ways to promote proficiency in the English language, the government... can promote proficiency in English by using it in its official actions and activities."[18] This means that city employees are "forbidden to translate documents into another language without official authorization."[19] Is this too much power for a local government to have? Chris Paige—

15   <www.wvwnews.net>
16   Ibid.
17   Dan Cheek, interview by Kenny Luck, 9 April 2010.
18   Hazleton City Counsel, *Official English Ordinance,* 8 September 2006.
19   Michael Powell and Michelle Garcia, "'They Must Leave,' Mayor of Hazleton Says After Signing Tough New Law," *The Washington Post*, 22 August 2006.

the candidate who ran against Barletta in the Republican primaries before dropping out in March 2010—thought so.

In a letter titled "Lou Barletta's Hazelton," Paige criticized Barletta for not being a true conservative. "Conservatives," Paige wrote, "believe in small government even if that means government is too small to eliminate illegal immigration."[20] It is a clever and consistent argument. Almost all conservatives are skeptical of a "large" government. But Paige is the only politician who consistently applies his conservatism to the "illegal immigration" debate. Barletta, on the other hand, while marching under the flag of conservatism, paradoxically did more to expand the reach of government power as mayor, while simultaneously bolstering his conservative credentials.

Less than two years after the Hazleton Ordinance passed, a Luzerne County Judge followed in Barletta's footsteps. Judge Peter Paul Olszewski, Jr.—who was voted out of the courtroom because of a questionable photo which surfaced during the 2009 campaign showing him in a Florida condo with corrupt former Judge Michael Conahan and a convicted drug dealer—ordered that four Spanish-speaking Hazleton men who pleaded guilty of robbery had to learn English as a punishment. As a March 2008 *Philadelphia Inquirer* article reported: "The unusual sentence requires that the [defendants] return to his court a year from now to take an English test and show that they can speak and write the language. If they fail, the men will have to serve the full two years of the four-to-24-month sentence that Olszewski imposed."[21] Olszewski imposed on the bench what Barletta

---

20   Chris Paige, "Lou Barletta's Hazelton," 7 December 2009. <www.pa2010.com/2009/12/lou-barlettas-hazleton>
21   Angela Couloumbis, "Judge Tells Defendants: Learn English 4 Spanish-

could not through the legislative process.

But the decision did not go without criticism. Witold Walczak, legal director of the ACLU of Pennsylvania, noted: "A big concern is the vagueness of the order to learn English—because what does that really mean? Does it mean you have to speak the King's English? Or read *Ulysses*?"[22] Mandating that immigrants learn English is without precedent in Pennsylvania. It can be argued that imposing such a decision perpetuates racial and ethnic stereotypes of immigrants. Deakos said that she and another Hazelton resident confronted Barletta, offered an alternative, but was ignored. "We went to the mayor. We printed out the immigration law and said, 'You should go and demand that these kids get deported,' " she recalled telling Barletta. "Not say that they should learn English."[23] Barletta dismissed Deakos' request.

The Lozano Case

Before the Hazelton ordinance could be enacted, its constitutionality was immediately challenged. In *Lozano v. Hazelton* (2007), the Federal District Court issued an injunction, and immediately declared the Hazelton ordinance invalid and unconstitutional. In a written decision, the court made clear that Hazelton's reasoning for enacting the ordinance, "flew in the face of long-established principles of constitutional law, not to mention the concept of justice." The Court added: "All persons in the United States have rights under the Fourteenth Amendment to the U.S.

---

speaking Hazleton Men Must Pass a Test to Avoid Jail Time," *The Philadelphia Inquirer*, 28 March 2008, sec. B.
22   Ibid.
23   Dee Deakos, interview by Kenny Luck, 5 May 2010.

Constitution, whether they are citizens or not."[24] Those in favor of upholding the city ordinance argued that "because illegal immigrants broke the law to enter the United States, they should not have any legal recourse when rights due them under the federal constitution or federal law are violated."[25]

In other words, the "illegal is illegal" mantra shouted by xenophobes fails to recognize that illegal or not, all persons in the United States are still subject to protection as "persons" under the 14th Amendment. In response, the court determined that Hazleton was itself breaking the law by intruding on the federal government's "role as supreme authority in regulating immigration." The law was then struck down, and Hazleton appealed to the Third Circuit Court of Appeals. [26]

In a striking blow to Barletta's anti-immigration crusade, the Third Circuit Court in September 2010 upheld Judge James Munley's 2007 decision that the Hazleton City Ordinance was unconstitutional. The appellate court made clear: "Whether Hazleton inadvertently stumbled into this exclusively federal domain, or decided to defiantly barge in, it is clear that it has attempted to usurp authority that the Constitution has placed beyond the vicissitudes of local governments."[27] In a sly political maneuver, while in the midst of a congressional campaign, Barletta vowed to appeal the decision again, calling the Third Circuit "the most

---

24   Lozano v. Hazelton, <u>United States Federal District Court,</u> 26 July 2007. <http://www.pamd.uscourts.gov/Lozano/decision.htm> (9 November 2008)
25   Ibid.
26   Michael Matza, "U.S. Appeals Court Hears Hazleton Case," *The Philadelphia Inquirer*, 31 October 2008.
27   Joe McDonald and Sam Galski, "Appeals Court Upholds Judge Munley's Ruling on Hazleton's Crackdown on Illegal Immigration," *The Times-Tribune*, 10 September 2010.

liberal court in America on immigration issues."[28] Now a congressman, Barletta has left for Washington, leaving Hazleton to deal with the financial and legal problems that he began. Four days after the November 2010 elections, *The Times Leader* reported that "an insurance company does not have to pay attorney's fees associated with Hazelton's City's battle over its illegal immigration ordinance, leaving the city on the hook for at least 2.4 million dollars."[29] This revelation came after The Third Circuit rejected Hazelton's argument that the city did not have to "pay for the legal fees of Pedro Lozano,"[30] one of the plaintiffs who sued Hazelton over its Illegal Immigration Relief Act in 2006. Speaking months before The Third Circuit's decision, Paige pointed out the problems with Barletta's court appeals. "A lot of people would agree with him on immigration in the abstract, but they would not agree going broke over it," he said, not knowing then that the city would later lose its court appeals. "Barletta's got this problem where the city could actually go broke over the lawsuit. It is a problem that looms at there."[31]

Deakos—who regularly attends city council meetings—also had concerns about Barletta's courts appeals, even before Hazelton lost both its court appeals in September and November 2010. "He knew he was going to open up the city to legal problems," she said. "He couldn't afford to go into it. There was a town in California and another one in Texas who backed off because they knew what it was going to cost. And for that reason alone it was really reckless, but it made

28　　Ibid.
29　　Terrie Morgan-Besecker, "Hazelton is Facing 2.4M Legal Bill," *The Times Leader*, 6 November 2010.
30　　Ibid.
31　　Chris Paige, interview by Kenny Luck, 17 May 2010.

Dan Check, who operates the blog www.StopLouBarletta.com, cites the following grievances against Barletta:

- As reported by the Citizen's Voice, Barletta accepted $1,000 in campaign contributions on March 28, 2008, from Paul DeAngelo, who in 1994 was sentenced for 18 months in jail for his involvement in a Luzerne County cocaine-distribution ring.

- Barletta has been endorsed by David Duke, a former member of the Ku Klux Klan leadership.

- As mayor of Hazleton, one of Barletta's first acts was to slash the police force in half. Barletta then blamed the resulting spike in crime on an "illegal immigrant crime wave."

- Barletta worked to pass one of the most extremist pieces of legislation in the country into law in Hazleton. The law, which drew wide-spread opposition from all quarters, was deemed unconstitutional by an US Federal Judge.

- Barletta illegally used Hazleton Pension Fund money, resulting in a massive financial problem for the city (one that might result in the city going bankrupt).

- Without proper authorization from Hazleton City Council, Barletta racked up millions of dollars in city debt trying to defend his Illegal Immigration Relief Act in Federal Court. After a court ruled that the city, and not its insurance company, is liable for that debt, Hazleton is on the verge of bankruptcy.

- Barletta's most recent budget for the city of Hazleton is chock full of huge tax hikes, city layoffs, and cuts in city financed programs. Worse, despite not receiving funding for this budget, Barletta is still pushing forward with it.

- As a political candidate, Barletta has proven inept at fundraising and has racked up massive personal debt.

"At one level he is saying he is a great financial manager, and at another level he's in The Standard Speaker almost every day saying Hazelton is almost broke. That juxtaposition is a problem for him."

—*Chris Paige*

him popular as hell."[32] What is more, Cheek also foresaw the financial problems Hazelton would face because of the mayor's continuous court appeals. "Barletta decided to appeal this, using city funds without any approval. It was never actually approved by the city council," he said. Rather, the former mayor "set up a small website called 'Small Town Defenders,' and the original intent was 'I am going to pay for this myself.' "[33] Some have questioned the validity and merit of "Small Town Defenders." Barletta originally conceived the idea after appearing on Lou Dobbs. "Dobbs gave him 10,000 dollars to start this fund, and he had money being sent to him for all over the county," Deakos explained. "The money was being sent to him, and really it should have been going to the city budget as a contribution. That is all questionable."[34] People sent Barletta money to fight illegal immigration and, as Deakos suggests, the money did not find its way into Hazleton's coffers. Rather, the money was dubiously used to fund Barletta's personal war against illegal immigration. It is not clear how much money Barletta has been given, and what that money has been used for. It is difficult to follow this up because, as Cheek points out, Barletta "hasn't updated the blog in about three years."[35]

The Aftermath

In Shenandoah, PA, a sleepy Appalachian town 20 miles from Hazelton, Luis Ramirez, a Mexican who had been in the United States illegally for six years, was beat to death in what some called an act of racist, anti-immi-

---

32 Dee Deakos, interview by Kenny Luck, 5 May 2010.
33 Dan Cheek, interview by Kenny Luck, 9 April 2010.
34 Dee Deakos, interview by Kenny Luck, 5 May 2010.
35 Dan Cheek, interview by Kenny Luck, 9 April 2010.

grant rage. Two white teenage boys—Derrick Donchak and Brandon Plekarsky—were charged with the crime before being acquitted less than one year later.[36] Controversy and outrage erupted over the verdict. In December 2009, the United States Department of Justice announced a number of indictments against a Federal Grand Jury and alleged police corruption in the case.[37] In October 2010, however, an all-white jury convicted Donchak and Plekarsky on all charges. Upon hearing the verdict, Crystal Dillman, Ramirez's fiancée, commented: "It's nice to know that there is some justice."[38]

Gladys Limon, a lawyer for the Mexican American Legal Defense and Education Fund, believes that "the inflammatory rhetoric in the immigration debate does have a correlation with increased violence against Latinos."[39] Whether this is true or not depends on how you answer this question: By enacting anti-immigration laws, does government encourage xenophobia and enable violence toward minorities and immigrants? Barletta does not think so. After expressing a rather phony, insincere display of sympathy over Ramirez's death, the former mayor added: "I don't believe our ordinance had anything to do with it. Every person is responsible for their own actions."[40] Perhaps, but what Barletta fails to recognize is that by targeting racial groups through legislation,[41] an explicit message is sent to the community

---

36   <http://www.huffingtonpost.com/2009/05/04/luis-ramirez-killers-foun_n_195535.html> (1 March 2010)

37   Ibid.

38   Joe McDonald, "Hate Crime: Guilty." *The Times-Tribune*, 15 October 2010.

39   Sean D. Hamill, "Mexican's Death Bares a Town's Ethnic Tension," *The New York Times*, 5 August 2008.

40   Ibid.

41   Although the Illegal Immigration Relief Act does not mention Latinos by name, let's be clear: No one is confused about who the city legislation is referring to. It is not as if Hazelton had a problem with too many immigrants from

that it is justified to fear and act against foreigners, as highlighted by the Ramirez beating and death.

In April 2010, the Arizona State Legislature passed an anti-immigration law which *The Economist* called an act of "hysterical nativism."[42] It resembled the Hazelton ordinance of 2006. Former *WILK* news commentator Kevin Lynn was outraged upon hearing the news of the new Arizona law. "This immigration thing going on down there in Arizona actually makes Lou Barletta look reasonable, which is reason enough to throw it out immediately," Lynn said. "I don't want to call it a processor because I would hate to give Lou Barletta any kind of credit. It is just a racist and bigoted thing that he started and now these people are perpetuating."[43] In May 2010, Hazelton City Council meeting, Councilwomen Karin Cabell—who had been barred from doing government contacts for 17 years before becoming a council member—suggested that, "in solidarity," Hazelton should send the Arizona State legislature a letter of support.[44] Barletta sat in attendance, with a smug look on his face. When asked what she thought about Cabell's proposal, Deakos insisted that sending the letter to Arizona "is one of those feel good things that they do."[45]

A lifelong Hazelton resident, Deakos acknowledges the problems Hazelton must confront. She pointed out how Barletta's management of Hazelton before leaving for Washington has made things worse. "As much as everybody

Canada.

42   <http://www.economist.com/world/united-states/displaystory. cfm?story_id=15954262>

43   Kevin Lynn, interview by Kenny Luck, 28 April 2010.

44   < https://www.epls.gov/epls/search.do?debar_recid=1682&status=arch ive&vindex=0&xref=true >

45   Dee Deakos, interview by Kenny Luck, 5 May 2010.

loves him for that illegal immigration act it was a negative thing for him to do," she observed. "It was so fiscally irresponsible on his part. He knew that he was going to get sued, and we didn't have the resources to fight it. That was reckless."[46]

---

46   Dee Deakos, interview by Kenny Luck, 5 May 2010.

two

The Luzerne County Christmas Display Incident

"It was really a legal argument but people wanted to make it into a religious one. People see my position as very hostile, but I suppose it is warranted in a way because this is what they have believed their entire lives, and if your beliefs are challenged people get angry."

—Justin Vacula, *King's College Student*

In early December 2009, the Luzerne County Courthouse erected its nativity scene in Wilkes-Barre, PA, a "tradition" that had endured for decades. The crèche, menorah and other symbols lay in display—paid for and maintained by county money—so that all could see.[47] Because the display had become customary, no one seemed to think it was illegal. Yet, the display raised a series of questions: With religious symbols paid

---

47   A letter sent on December 11, 2009, from the ACLU of Pennsylvania also noted that "the crèche is also illuminated at night, thus making it yet more prominent as a standalone religious display."

for and displayed by government, was this not an endorsement of religion? Was this display constitutional?

Justin Vacula, a junior at nearby King's College, questioned the display's constitutionality and contacted the American Civil Liberties Union (ACLU) to see what could be done. On December 11, 2009, the ACLU sent Commissioners Petrilla, Skrepenak, and Urban a letter. Witold Walczak, Legal Director of the ACLU of Pennsylvania, informed the commissioners that "both displays violate the Establishment Clause of the First Amendment of the U.S. Constitution,"[48] and asked that it be removed immediately. The ACLU added: "Because of the clear constitutional violation posed by these religious symbols," if the county commissioners did not respond by December 18, the ACLU will "have no choice but to seek relief from a federal judge."[49] A lawsuit loomed, while a debate over the role and reach of religious involvement in Luzerne County was about to take place.

Vacula is a member of the NEPA Free Thought Society, an activist group that describes itself as a "coalition of unbelievers comprised of atheists, secular humanists, skeptics, agnostics, and rationalists,"[50] who hold monthly meetings to discuss religion and politics. Founded in November 2007, the group has roughly 100 members,[51] which pales in comparison to many of the church congregations in Northeastern Pennsylvania. The NEPA Free Thinkers are a minority in the region; moreover, with a landscape filled with ethno-religious groups such as Irish, Italian,

---

48   < http://www.aclu.org/religion-belief/pennsylvania-county-agrees-remove-religious-symbols-courthouse-lawn>
49   Ibid.
50   <http://www.meetup.com/NEPA-Freethought>
51   Ibid. As of March 2010.

and Polish Catholics—not to mention various Protestant churches—the Free Thinkers are a group with little social or political influence. But that would change with Vacula's public challenge to the government of Luzerne County.

Adding to the suspense and drama, the county commissioners waited until the day before the ACLU deadline, December 17, to remove the Christmas display. They complied with the ACLU's request reluctantly. Commissioner Steve Urban, as reported by the *Times-Tribune*, commented: "I think the people of this county are outraged and rightfully so."[52] People *were* outraged, although, surprisingly, not outraged enough to challenge the ACLU's stance.

A Clear Constitutional Violation

County Solicitor Vito DeLuca said the reason Luzerne County did not pursue the case was because "of a local budget crisis and other pressing matters."[53] What DeLuca did not mention, however, was that challenging the ACLU would probably involve lengthy litigation, costing the county hundreds of thousands of dollars, which would most likely end in defeat. "A myth that was going around was that there was this lawsuit going on, but there was never any lawsuit filed," Vacula said. "The sentiment at the courthouse was that they complied. They obviously did not fight it. There was no need to because it was that simple."[54] Lu-

52   Coulter Jones, "Courthouse pulls nativity, menorah display to avoid lawsuit," *The Times-Tribune*, 18 December 2009
<http://citizensvoice.com/news/courthouse-pulls-nativity-menorah-displays-to-avoid-lawsuit-1.495916>
53   The Associated Press. "Commissioners Remove Holiday Items from Luzerne County Courthouse Lawn," 17 December 2009
<http://www.pennlive.com/midstate/index.ssf/2009/12/holiday_items_removed_from_luz.html>
54   Justin Vacula, interview by Kenny Luck, 2 March 2010.

zerne County did not have a particularly strong argument to keep the religious display on the lawn. "What they did to make it right," Vacula explained, "was that they made it inclusive. They made it into a Holiday Display instead of a Christian Display. They added a lot of other decorations."[55]

A Wall of Separation

The December 11 ACLU letter cited several important court precedents to support their argument against displaying the crèche and the menorah. As established in *County of Allegheny v. ACLU* (1989), "A public entity may display a religious symbol, if at all, only when the symbol is integrated into a broader display that, taken all together, communicates a secular message to viewers."[56] The Luzerne County Courthouse display did not pass this test. But religiously devout disagreed. They argued that if government does not endorse a religious message, that somehow is an infringement on their right to freely practice their faith. In other words, by removing the clearly illegal governmentally endorsed symbols, their beliefs are under "attack" by secular rationalists and government officials.

> **"You can't just have this unrestricted power and think that you are above the law. In too many cases, religion wants to be above the law saying, 'We don't have to listen to these rules.'"**
>
> **—Justin Vacula**

---

55   Ibid.
56   < http://www.aclu.org/religion-belief/pennsylvania-county-agrees-remove-religious-symbols-courthouse-lawn>

In an article titled, "The Constitutional Fight over Holiday Symbols, and the So-Called 'War on Christmas,' " Marcia Hamilton cogently explored the Christmas display debate. "Those who use the phrase 'War on Christmas' in this context," she argued, "mean to suggest that the constitutional constraints on the ability of the government to endorse religious symbols and messages are an attack on Christmas." Hamilton, adding for good measure, noted: "if there is any war being waged during the contemporary holiday season, it is a 'War on Non-believers' by Christians."[57] It is not as if the government is prohibiting any individuals from practicing their own religion, displaying symbols of their faith, or anything else. What offends these religious crusaders is the absence of an endorsed religion from government. Their argument confuses the right *to* practice religion with the right to be protected *from* an endorsed religion.

Those who argue that the United States is somehow a "Christian Nation," simply do not understand history and American jurisprudence. Religion is only mentioned twice in the United States Constitution. In article VI's Religious Test Clause ("No religious test shall ever be required as a Qualification to any Office or public Trust under the United States") and the Establishment Clause of the First Amendment ("Congress shall make no law respecting an establishment of religion, or prohibiting the free exercise thereof"). Those who try to substantiate the erroneous premise that the United States is a theocracy have a serious burden of proof to demonstrate. It is simply not enough that the pil-

---

57   Maria Hamilton, "The Constitutional Fight Over Holiday Symbols, and the So-Called 'War on Christmas,' Find Law, 24 December 2009.
<www.writnews.findlaw.com/hamilton/20091224.html

grims practiced Christianity generations before the United States was established. In addition, if the framers wanted an established state religion (England), or religion to actually *be* the government, such as in the case of a theocracy (post-1979 Iran), then why be so indirect? Why not just make it clear? Why not include a clause such as: "The official religion of the United States shall be Christianity. All citizens are required to adhere to, and support this creed"?[58] If one reads the Constitution the answers to these questions are clear. But when the ACLU challenged Luzerne County on the constitutionality of the display, surprisingly, those who supported keeping the display, without modifications, did not use the obvious line of reasoning: The display did not constitute an established religion (as prohibited by the Establishment Clause) and could therefore remain on the lawn. This argument would have probably failed to save the display because it would have violated the precedent set in *County of Allegheny v. ACLU*, but it would have been at least rational. Their arguments, often seen in editorials and heard on talk radio, were far more absurd. In the minds of some believers, Thomas Jefferson's "wall of separation" was not a wall at all, but a secular hurdle to be jumped and knocked down.

---

58   The South Carolina Constitution of 1778 did, in fact, establish a religion. Article 38 states: "...all persons and religious societies who acknowledge that there is one God, and a future state of rewards and punishments, and that God is publicly to be worshipped, shall be freely tolerated. The Christian Protestant religion shall be deemed, and is hereby constituted and declared to be, the established religion of this State." No clause ever remotely resembled anything like this in the federal constitution.

Radical Reactions

"Get a life. Luzerne County has enough problems. Don't create any more. COMMUNIST!" —*Bill C.*

"…You ARE one of the most hated people in the valley." —*Kate W.*

"You are a [expletive] homo. A nativity scene does not persecute any religion. It's a [expletive] American tradition. Are you a Nazi? — *Mason W.*

"You [are] a worthless human being." —*Jim T. (from email)*

"May God have pity on your empty soul before you burn in hell for your defiant, blatant, antagonistic acts of heresy and blasphemy!" —*Brian A. (from email)*

"It ain't [expletive] unconstitutional! You dumb [expletive]! … now shut the [expletive] up and crawl back into your hole…" – *Amanda S.*

"I hope they shoot you." —*Phil M.*

"[Expletive] the constitution if it's that serious. Why do dollars say IN GOD WE TRUST?" —*Anarie R. (from email)*

"You are a wart on society's ass." —*Frank W.*

"Now go somewhere else and cause some controversy… like go escort girls at an abortion clinic… so that they can safely 'choose' to kill their own flesh and blood… go speak at a gay rights convention." —*Tim C*

http://greenatheist.blogspot.com/2010/02/hate-mail-montage-from-december.html

Radical Reactions

Many religious advocates responded with venomous insults when Luzerne County complied with the ACLU request. Vacula, who by the middle of December became a local celebrity, was bitterly attacked by his opponents. "There was a ton of hostility," Vacula said. "I felt threatened in many cases that people were going to come after me."[59] Many of Vacula's detractors offered anti-intellectual, irrational arguments in support of their position. Most of the arguments aimed at Vacula were merely *ad hominem* attacks *disguised* as arguments. Take, for example, WKRZ DJ Jumpin' Jeff Walker. During a radio appearance on December 18, 2009, the sun-baked radio host, who admits to being turned off by "bleeding-heart liberals,"[60] blasted Vacula for attending a religious college. "I gave my reasons for why I did it," Vacula explained, "and Jeff Walker just kept going on and on."[61] What was Walker trying to prove? Does Vacula's status at a religious college somehow excuse the county government from breaking the law? Is such an observation even relevant? Walker's petty quibbling misses the point. By diverting attention away from the real issue (whether or not Luzerne County's display violated the Establishment Clause) and attacking Vacula's attendance at a religious college, Walker offered no other tenable argument.

When examining the positions of Vacula's detractors, a high level of hypocrisy is quite noticeable. One the one hand, many religious devotees claim to be tolerant and peaceful toward others. But that was not true in this case. Of the

59   Justin Vacula, interview by Kenny Luck, 2 March 2010.
60   <http://www.985krz.com/pages/4753564.php#jeff>
61   Justin Vacula, interview by Kenny Luck, 2 March 2010.

roughly 1,500 hostile messages Vacula received, a majority were from so-called devout individuals—people who attend church often and maintain a strong belief in God. According to Vacula, his attackers were not radical fanatics but average church-goers, and that is what makes this such a striking case. "A common sentiment I hear is that the moderates aren't doing anything bad, and that these people aren't dangerous," Vacula explained. "But these people who got in touch with me were the moderates. These are the 'Average Joe' religious people of Luzerne County."[62]

Happy Holidays?

By the time Christmas arrived things began to settle down. A new, modified display was erected, paid for by donations from a local law firm, and everyone seemed to win. The new display was now secularized by including religious and non-religious figures.

The Luzerne County Christmas Display Incident is emblematic of how nasty some people can become when involved in a debate over religion. "It obviously did make people unhappy," Vacula admitted, "but it was illegal." During an appearance on *WBRE Morning News*, Mary Roper, an ACLU representative, claimed that Vacula was not the first to question the constitutionality of the display, but he was the only one willing to take a stand publicly. It is a decision he does not regret. "Good things did come from this, and I hope that we will do the right thing next year," Vacula said. "Other violations just won't happen again."[63]

---

62   Ibid.
63   Ibid.

three

King Corbett

"Tune into WILK 'Fox News Junior' with fake liberal Steve Corbett."

—Dan Spak, *Blogger*

When former *Times Leader* columnist Steve Corbett resigned from his job in 2002 to move to California, he was probably unaware that within five years, he would be back in Northeastern Pennsylvania, provoking debate and causing controversy as the host of *WILK*'s *Corbett*. "I realized that the media and political culture was flat where I was," he said.[64] In recent years, however, Corbett is perhaps known best for his support of right-wing political figures such as Sarah Palin and his opposition to President Barack Obama. As a self-proclaimed liberal, who "flip-flopped" during the 2008 presidential election, Corbett has alienated many center-left individuals while simultaneously endorsing many right-wing politicians in the name of supporting "good government."

---

64   Steve Corbett, interview by Kenny Luck, 12 April 2010.

One can argue that many of Corbett's positions are flat-out contradictory. And although he urges that a person "has to have facts from which to draw conclusions,"[65] the conclusions that he usually draws, on the other hand, seem based on pure speculation; are personal attacks disguised as arguments; or take form in his unquestioned ability to incite a populist rage from many of his sycophantic callers. These observations have prompted many sensible people to question his aims. "I don't disagree with the fact that he is smart, and well-read, but it is his opinion, as is in any talk show," said Evie Rafalko McNulty, Lackawanna County Recorder of Deeds and former County Commissioner candidate. "When you argue with him he says, 'Ok, we are out, we are going on a break.' He did that to me once before, and I thought to myself, 'Ok, you're not getting me again.' He has been challenged before, and people have offered to go down there and argue with him in the studio. But no, he never takes you up on that. He won't share the airwaves. Not when he can control it with the flip of a button."[66]

Corbett sees himself as an anti-corruption crusader and liberal feminist. Yet, above all, he believes that through his radio show he is contributing to the greater public good—a claim that has been challenged. Duke Barrett, a frequent *WILK* caller known to listeners as "Duke from Dallas," maintains that Corbett is not really a journalist in the conventional sense, but a political pundit. "I find Corbett not to be a journalist *per se*. He is what I would say a commentator where he has all sorts of sources about local goings-on, but he strikes me to be contrary just to be contrary."[67]

---

65   Ibid.
66   Evie Rafalko McNulty, interview by Kenny Luck, 1 April 2010.
67   Duke Barrett, interview by Kenny Luck, 25 April 2010.

Presidential Politics

During the 2008 primary and general election campaign cycles, Corbett's show became a Barack-bashing symposium *par excellence*. "A lot of these people who support Barack Obama seem blinded by his mystique," he said. "There are people who hate me because I oppose Barack Obama. I was supposed to be the guy who was Barack Obama's ally."[68] Whatever mystique Obama allegedly has, Corbett is not blinded by it.

During the 2008 primary election cycle, the news commentator incessantly talked about Obama's smoking habit, insisting that the then Senator can "do a lot of good by talking publicly about kicking his habit."[69] Here, Corbett was disguising petty pandering as some sort of altruistic greater good.

"He likes to find little things to nitpick that he finds important which I think—and probably the general public thinks—are minutia," Barrett said. As a regular caller who appears on many *WILK* programs, Barrett recognizes the approach Corbett often uses to incite controversy on his show. "If it's a dig on a progressive or liberal politician then a majority of the listeners who tend to lean conservative are all over that kind of thing. I find that kind of discussion completely ridiculous because it might get good ratings, but does nothing to further the discussion on a serious level."[70]

In addition to discussing Obama's bad personal habits, Corbett also berated the former senator for not hiring union workers during his campaign, and called attention

68   Steve Corbett, interview by Kenny Luck, 12 April 2010.
69   Steve Corbett, "Barack Kicks Butt," WILK FM, 21 March 2008.
< http://wilknetwork.com/Barack-Kicks-Butt/1866562> (8 November 2008)
70   Duke Barrett, interview by Kenny Luck, 25 April 2010.

to Obama's alleged sexist attitude (prompted by his calling one woman "sweetie").[71]

When former Senator Clinton, the candidate who Corbett enthusiastically supported, lost the Democratic primaries in June 2008, he then backed Senator John McCain, a Republican. But something did not add up: How could a self-proclaimed die-hard liberal feminist back a conservative Republican? McNulty offered a possible answer. "Steve is in a business where controversy sells," she said, attempting to explain Corbett's conservative switch. "He was not going to be able to incite fear, and incite arguments, and controversy, for being for what the Democrats were for."[72]

In an article titled, "Local Clinton Backers, McCain Advisor Meet," the Scranton *Times-Tribune* reported that McCain's economic advisor and former HP Chairwomen, Carly Fiorina, had met on August 18, 2008 at the home of Jamie Brazil in Dunmore to discuss and plan their opposition to Obama's candidacy. In attendance that day was Tony Rodham, Hillary Clinton's younger brother.[73] Through a series of controversies, Rodham has been an embarrassment to the Clintons, and is considered by many to be a political liability for his older sister.[74]

Among his many screw-ups, Rodham was involved with an assault episode in August 2001; he could not afford to pay alimony and child support to his former wife Nicole Boxer in late 2007; and he entered into a multi-million

---

71   < http://bigdanblogger.blogspot.com/2008/06/nepas-feminist-fraud-ster-wilks-steve.html (20 June 2008)>
72   Evie Rafalko McNulty, interview by Kenny Luck, 1 April 2010.
73   Borys Krawczeniuk, "Local Clinton Backers, McCain Advisor Meet," *The Times-Tribune,* 20 August 2008.
74   Michael Kranish, "Pardons Reemerge as Issue in Clinton Run," *The Boston Globe,* 28 February 2007.

dollar business deal in 1999 to grow and export hazelnuts from the Republican of Georgia. That plan made National Security Advisor Sandy Berger upset when it was revealed that Rodham's "local connection in Batumi turned out to be Aslan Abashidze, a major political opponent of Georgian President Eduard Shevardnadze, a key U.S. ally in the region."[75] It is well-known that the Rodham family has deep connections to Northeastern Pennsylvania, and Corbett is friends with good ol' Tony. As part of Rodham's circle of acquaintance, Corbett is often invited to inner-circle gatherings when Rodham is in town. And although he did not attend the August 18 meeting in Dunmore, by his own admission, Corbett has been to similar Republican political gatherings. "I was up at wherever they had it in the hotel in Clarks Summit. I was there for that," he said. "It is no secret that that's what I supported."[76]

According to McNulty: "Steve's been carrying the Rodham water because he is always invited to little inner-circle kind of things."[77] When Rodham threw his weight behind McCain, Corbett followed. This observation has also been articulated by blogger Dan Spak, who has devoted much time writing about Corbett on his blog *"Big Dan's Big Blog"* (www.bigdanblogger.blogspot.com). "I think maybe that part of the reason he went to Palin," Spak explained, "was a reaction that Obama beat his good buddies, the Rodhams."[78]

After hearing about Rodham's and Corbett's conservative conversion in the summer, McNulty commented to a local newspaper: "Poor Hillary. You can pick your friends,

75 < http://en.wikipedia.org/wiki/Tony_Rodham>
76 Steve Corbett, interview by Kenny Luck, 12 April 2010.
77 Evie Rafalko McNulty, interview by Kenny Luck, 1 April 2010.
78 Dan Spak, interview by Kenny Luck, 12 April 2010.

but you can't pick your family" (referencing the political flip flop committed by both Corbett and Rodham). Mc-Nulty says, irked by the remark, Corbett called her and commented: "Is it because you didn't get the job to run the Hillary headquarters?"[79] She suspects that the only reason Corbett would ask such a question is because he was taking his talking points from Rodham. "At that point I thought to myself, 'Shame on them,'" she said. "You don't jump the ship and all of a sudden change your morals, political beliefs, and philosophies—they don't change after a concession speech for God's sake," she said. "I still stand by that."

Another revealing observation is Corbett's connection with Fiorina. Virtually ignored by the Obama campaign, the radio commentator opened his doors to the McCain campaign via Fiorina. "She's been in the studio and she's the one who broke the McCain buzz here, and of course I did not turn her away," he said.[80] Fiorina spoke at the Republican National Convention. "She was on the air with him, she called the show," McNulty said. "It all mattered, I'm telling you, by where he was invited, and who called his show."[81] Is this why Corbett insisted on "not turning Fiorina away"?

The Polls

In the weeks leading up to the presidential election on November 4, 2008, Corbett mistakenly received an internal email sent by Grant Olin who operated the Wilkes-Barre headquarters of the Obama Campaign.[82] According

79   Evie Rafalko McNulty, interview by Kenny Luck, 1 April 2010.
80   Steve Corbett, interview by Kenny Luck, 12 April 2010.
81   Evie Rafalko McNulty, interview by Kenny Luck, 1 April 2010.
82   Oujdi, "Rumor: Obama's Internals in PA Apparently Leaked," *Daily Kos*, 14 October 2008. <http://www.dailykos.com/storyon-

to media sources, the email went to 627 supporters report-ing that an internal poll had shown Obama leading by only two points in Pennsylvania.[83] Based upon this information, Obama's lead was well within the margin of error and, ac-cording to Corbett, the election was "in a dead heat."

A Gallup Daily Tracking Poll—conducted between October 25 and 27—was the poll Corbett cited. The news commentator doubted the polls, but arbitrarily used the one poll which was advantageous to his political position. Among 11 national polls, it was the only one which had Obama at such a low margin over McCain.[84] And there was a reason: its methodology was flawed.

On October 25, a few days before the election, pollster Paul Maslin recognized the problem with the polls. He noted: "The 'likely' voter model offered by Gallup is flawed. The Gallup organization itself seems to recognize this, since it is also reporting an 'expanded' turnout model that has Obama running anywhere from two to four net points better than its 'traditional' model." Maslin continued: "The flaw is simple: Gallup identifies 'likely' voters by asking their previous voting history, meaning that if you are first-time voter or you skipped voting in either 2000 or 2004, your preference is either not counted at all or weighed down."[85] To repeat, Gallup's "likely" voter model had the race within the margin of error with Obama at 49 percent and McCain at 47 percent.[86] What is more, the poll failed to take into ac-

---

ly/2008/10/15/05041/703/752/630799> (10 November 2008)

83   Ibid.

84   Paul Maslin, "Obama's Big Lead in the Polls is Real," *Salon.com*, 25 Octo-ber 2008 <http://www.salon.com/opinion/feature/2008/10/25/obamas_lead/ > (10 November 2008)

85   Ibid.

86   Ibid.

COMMON CORBETT FALLACIES

The Straw Man

The Straw Man is an old debating trick. It occurs when in the midst of an argument one side deliberately distorts the other person's position, and then proceeds to attack the distortion. If you listen closely, you could spot this fallacy often on Corbett.

Red Herring

When the Mayor of Scranton announced his bid for governor in November 2009, Corbett was there, red herring and all. After complaining about how traffic was stopped in the downtown, Corbett wrote how Mayor Doherty did not ask for a "moment of silence for Brenda Williams, the mentally-ill Air Force veteran who died at the trigger fingers of Scranton cops." A sad and controversial subject for sure, but what relevance does it have in the middle of an election bid for governor? If Doherty had evoked the spirit of Brenda Williams, I am sure Corbett would have lambasted the mayor for capitalizing off the memory of Brenda Williams for political gain.

Lack of Evidence

Corbett often makes sweeping conclusions based primarily on fragmented pieces of information. On June 2, 2008, when it seemed clear that Hillary Clinton would not be the Democratic Party nominee, he argued,"…without them [white, female voters] democrats will rally around a flawed candidate who will further divide the party into have's and have-not's." In this case, his conclusion was wrong because his premise was assumed. Corbett failed to cite any polls that would confirm this assumption. As history would show, the white female demographic did not leave the Democratic Party in hordes during the 2008 general election as he maintained.

Narrowly Framed Issues

Defining what the issue is "really about" puts Corbett in control of the discussion. How many times have we heard him say, "That's not what I'm talking about," when really, it is? By selecting the perimeters of a topic, Corbett can, and at times does, delegitimize an opponent by making their argument seem irrelevant within the framework he himself constructs.

Loaded Questions

Corbett urges us to "ask more questions and don't back off." Yet all questions are not created equal. The types of questions asked can influence the answerer, and that commonly happens on Corbett. In an October 2009 interview, Scranton City Counsel Candidate Doug Miller walked right down the path Corbett laid out for him. Afterwards, Corbett claimed that the questions he asked were "fair." A number of callers contested this claim.

Ad Hominem Attacks

Attack the person, not his or her position. This is the ad hominem fallacy. Although rarely used by Corbett, this tactic does make an appearance from time to time. In most instances, Corbett uses it subtly by making a caricature of his opponent. The use of tone or the embellishment of certain words while speaking also creates this effect. Consider Corbett's use of tone while criticizing Cory O'Brian: "O'Brien looks in the mirror and sees nothing and nobody but himself" (October 2009).

count the massive new voter registration conducted by the Democrats that year. The accuracy of the 'traditional' model was called into question, yet Corbett failed to mention any of this on the air. Despite all the evidence to the contrary, Corbett continued to insist that Obama would lose. Looking back, he seemed to be taking his talking points straight from the McCain/Palin command center. With respect to the polls, there are two likely possibilities which could accurately explain Corbett's flawed analysis. First, he simply was not aware that the poll's methodology was flawed and, as a result, could not call its validity into question. Second, he knew the former but deliberately chose to ignore the available facts. Whatever the truth, Corbett was wrong, and the empirical data confirm this. Richard Kulka, Ph.D., of the Kansas-based American Association of Public Opinion Research, made clear in the days shortly after the election that all of the polls were "on the mark."[87] Dr. Kulka's group asserted: "The overall national popular vote was well within the margin of error. Most were within a percentage point. The second thing," he added, "is that even in taking the state polls there were very few surprises."[88] As for Luzerne and Lackawanna Counties, Corbett's broadcasting region and the areas where he insisted Obama didn't stand a chance, had the highest turnout for the Democrat outside of Philadelphia and the second highest in the state.[89]

A few days after the election, Corbett wrote: "Even though my candidates went down in defeat at the polls, I

---

87 Borys Krawczeniuk, "Results within Error Margins," *The Scranton Times-Tribune,* 7 November 2008.
88 Ibid.
89 Robert Swift, "Obama Strongly Carries Lackawanna, Luzerne," *The Citizen's Voice,* 5 November 2008.

walked away from Election Day a winner."[90] He went on to explain that as long as you stand on principle, you will always win. But was it "principle" Corbett was standing on, or a heap of his own accumulated bull?

A Commitment to Commentary

Corbett often refers to himself as a "member of the press." Yet, by his own account, he remains biased. On October 3, 2008, while arguing with a woman live on radio about the upcoming presidential election he openly stated: "Don't think for one second that I am not supposed to take sides." When asked about the lack of objectivity on his show, in his usual pompous arrogance, Corbett restated his previous remarks: "If you want objectivity you came to the wrong guy. There is no objectivity," he said without hesitation. "As a commentator I take sides. I've got dozens of Keystone Awards in boxes in my attic that say 'News Column.' A column is commentary. I've broken news in commentary. I also believe that there is a whole hell of a lot of so-called straight up and down journalists—reporters—who don't really understand that there is very little objectivity in the craft. Anybody who tries to tarnish me by saying, 'His objectivity is at issue,' yeah, they're right. I am glad that they're paying attention."[91]

The problem is that Corbett merges commentary and news in a very unprincipled way, entangling fact and opinion. Mixing news and commentary may seem harmless, but it becomes a problem when someone's reputation is on the line. For instance, when Luzerne County Senior Judge

90   Steve Corbett, "Yes We Can," WILK FM, 7 November 2008
<http://wilknetwork.com/Yes-We-Can/3277985> (10 November 2008)
91   Steve Corbett, interview by Kenny Luck, 12 April 2010.

Chester Muroski was involved in a car accident in early January 2010, Corbett spent days making inferences and drawing quick conclusions about the nature of the incident even before the specifics of the accident were known publically. Although Muroski told a *Times Leader* reporter that he may have had "one, maybe two"[92] drinks, Corbett continued to insist that Muroski somehow broke the law, and that the judge should resign, even though Muroski was not charged with any crime.

Corbett engaged in character assassination against Muroski, smearing his reputation, and one would think that the radio host would be cautious when attacking someone publically without providing convincing evidence. He posed the question to his listeners: "Do you think Muroski

MEMORABLE MOMENTS

Thomas G. Krattenmaker, a professor of communications law at Georgetown University Law School, called Corbett's 1989 interview with murderer Glenn Wolsieffer "rash and imprudent" because Corbett failed to tell Wolsieffer that he was recording the interview. According to a December 1991 New York Times article, Corbett "violat[ed] a state law that prohibits the taping of a phone conversation without the consent of both parties." However, these charges were later dropped.

---

92   Edward Lewis, "Murokski Involved In Crash" *The Times Leader,* 5 January 2010. <http://www.timesleader.com/news/Muroski-involved-in-car-crash-.html > (5 January 2010)

should resign?" while insisting the entire time that he should. And although Corbett continually insists that the platform he provides on his show is not gossip-based, his verbal assault against Muroski was a clear example of news commentator's hypocrisy.

Other variables, such as bad weather and icy road conditions, were not taken into consideration by the news commentator, even though two fatal car accidents occurred on the same stretch of road within the same month as Muroski's crash. Corbett seemed to be aware of this, but it did not mitigate the attacks. [93] The conclusions he had drawn, however, were purely speculative, and implied that alcohol was the reason Muroski had crashed his car. If Corbett claimed to be reporting, guesswork and filling in the holes from one's own interpretation, instead of established facts, was bad journalism.

In an article titled, "Corbett Calls Muroski Defenders 'Brainwashed' and 'Demented,' " Steve Urbanski cogently argued the problems with Corbett's position. "No matter how badly Corbett wants to believe that Muroski was 'driving drunk,' the facts simply do not support his wild speculation," Urbanski wrote. "Corbett is certainly entitled to this own opinion, as are his listeners, but neither Corbett nor his listeners are entitled to their own facts."[94] According to Urbanski, witness Adam Swartwood said that Muroski was "absolutely not" drunk at the time of the accident.[95] Urbanski cited the Pennsylvania Vehicle Code, and quoted a witness to support his conclusion. Corbett, by contrast,

---

93   < http://www.wilknetwork.com/Saves-Lives--Don-t-Mourn-Lives/6106140> (4 April 2010)
94   Steve Urbanski, "Corbett Calls Muroski Defenders 'Brainwashed' and 'Demented,'" *Scranton Public Policy Examiner*, 7 January 2010.
95   Ibid.

relied on smear and second-hand hearsay. This example is important because it illustrates how when little is known about an event, gossip and speculation still manage to gain control of public discourse. The Muroski incident managed to show just how a pundit can hide behind a veneer of neutrality while still maintaining a hard bias toward an issue. In the Corbett Court of Public Opinion, Muroski was assumed guilty and had to be proven innocent.

You Better [NOT] Listen!

"I don't really think, in order to gain anything in this world, we need Steve Corbett calling himself a feminist," said McNulty. "We could do it on our own. And that goes for any man."[96] Corbett often claims to support left-of-center, liberal politics. This includes feminism, a favorable attitude toward immigrants, and First Amendment rights. "My politics are predominately left-wing politics," he said.[97] But why does he contradict himself, and his alleged progressive beliefs, by often endorsing Republican candidates? It is confusing, not courageous. "Just because you have a long grey pony tail doesn't mean you are a liberal," said Spak, commenting on the inconsistency of Corbett's positions. "He's not fooling anybody."[98] On his blog, Spak suggests that when Corbett endorsed the McCain/Palin ticket in 2008, he betrayed his feminist values. "I called him a 'feminist fraudster' because he was for Hillary, and then when Hillary got knocked out, he immediately went for Palin, and you can't get more right-wing than Sarah Palin," Spak explained. "She pales in comparison from Hillary

---

96   Evie Rafalko McNulty, interview by Kenny Luck, 1 April 2010.
97   Steve Corbett, interview by Kenny Luck, 12 April 2010.
98   Dan Spak, interview by Kenny Luck, 12 April 2010.

with woman's rights."

Corbett denies these claims and maintains that blogging is generally not a legitimate form of media. "A lot of these bloggers are wannabe newspaper columnists," he said. "A lot these bloggers like to believe that they have paid their dues, and they haven't. They have taken a personal dislike to me. But they are really wasting their own creativity, their own energy, their own pursuit of intellectual success by personally attacking me."[99]

In the face of these criticisms from Spak and others, Corbett continues to insist that he is, indeed, a liberal. He maintains that, although he disagreed with 90 percent of what McCain and Palin stood for, the other ten percent was important enough for him to support. Despite his "left wing politics," race was apparently not an important factor, as it was for many progressives during the 2008 election, in his voting. "I did not need to vote for Barack Obama as the first African-American president in the United States. I already voted for a black dude. I voted for Jesse Jackson twice," he commented. "I know about great black visionaries. Barack Obama is no great black visionary. I give fits to these so-called liberals because they are not really liberals."

As a committed liberal, however, Spak disagrees with Corbett's definition of "liberalism." He pointed out the problem with Corbett's position. "If you notice, he never bashes Republicans. He'll say, 'I wrote an article about racism once.' What, a long time ago? Where is that article about racism? In other words, he won't talk about racism in quantity. He won't devote a whole show or week to racism. He'll say, 'Once I voted for Jesse Jackson a long time ago. I

---

99   Steve Corbett, interview by Kenny Luck, 12 April 2010.

am a liberal.' But that does not make you a liberal. What are you doing right now? That's what counts."

Spak's observations are extremely important because they shed insight on the difficult problem of Corbett's contradictorily political positions. Often times, the news commentator claims to uphold some vague resemblance of progressive values, yet cites only his writing of an article in the distant past of evidence of his commitment to these ideals. For example, during an interview he noted: "There aren't a lot of newspaper columnists who wrote as much about race, bigotry, and racism than I did," he said. Yet if that were true, why spend so much time attacking people and politicians who, at least symbolically (i.e. Barack Obama, Paul Kanjorski), oppose racism and bigotry? Instead, he says that he and former Hazelton Mayor Lou Barletta, probably the leading bigot in Northeast Pennsylvania, "get along real fine."[100] Where is the righteous indignation? If Corbett's claims about liberalism were true, why did he not seize the opportunity and come out stronger against Barletta, in 2008 and 2010, making relevant his position on racism in a current context?[101]

Many people, including former colleagues, believe that Corbett's influence is marginal. "I don't think that he is representative of anything other than what Steve Corbett thinks," explained Kevin Lynn, who spent eight years as host of *The Morning News with Nancy and Kevin* on *WILK*.[102] Others, such as Spak, echo Lynn's sentiment. "He has no

---

100   Ibid.
101   To be fair, in February 2008, Corbett wrote an article titled, "Is Barletta's Glass Half Full or Half Empty?" The article was written early in the campaign, and was one of the few examples of Corbett criticizing Barletta. If Corbett truly did disagree with Barletta, the point was surely underemphasized in his writings.
102   Kevin Lynn, interview by Kenny Luck, 28 April 2010.

integrity. I think he will go wherever his name gets bigger," Spak argued. "Corbett thinks he is superior because he has a radio show, but that's the old media and the new media is the internet."[103]

Despite the criticism against his approach to news and politics, Corbett stubbornly insists that his work is important, influential, and fair. "Good journalism, people know it when they see it," he explained. "Bad journalism—they know that too."[104] Whether Corbett's work falls into the former or latter category remains to be seen. But in the end, when it comes to loud diatribes and personal bombast, one thing is certain: CORBETT IS KING.

103   Dan Spak, interview by Kenny Luck, 12 April 2010.
104   Steve Corbett, interview by Kenny Luck, 12 April 2010.

four

DeNaples's Veneer

"You don't want to mess with them. They are Louie De-Naples' cousins, and they own half of Scranton. I would get you and your friends and leave."
—**Bouncer,** *Trax Bar & Grille at the Radisson*

Twenty one year-old college student Dick Dewitt (who requested that his real name not be used) was enjoying a quiet evening of drinks with his friends at the Radisson Bar and Grille in Scranton one night in early March 2011. The bar was festive, filled with couples having drinks, people talking, and loud music. At one point, Dewitt asked a friend for a piece of gum. "Sorry, I don't have any," his peer answered. Then, a man walked past Dewitt's table. Dewitt leaned forward and tapped the man on the shoulder. "Hey, do you have a piece of gum?" he asked. Wearing a black leather coat and looking quite angry, the unidentified man paused and turned toward Dewitt. "What the *[expletive]* are you touching me for?" he said.

Dewitt had crossed paths with a member of one of Scranton's most notorious families. "The next thing I know," Dewitt said, "some 45 year old man is up in my face. 'I don't appreciate you touching me,' he said. 'You have no idea who the *[expletive]* you are messing with'."[105] Another man approached Dewitt. He stood next to the leather-clad individual who was offended, presumably because a college student had asked him for a piece of gum. After a few moments of insults and verbal profanity, which began to draw attention from the surrounding crowd, the two men disappeared. Then, a bouncer—dressed in a suit, looking elegant—approached the table and pulled Dewitt aside. "Look," he said, "I can throw you out of here, but I can't touch them. They are Louie DeNaples' cousins, and they own half of Scranton." The bouncer added, "If I throw them out, they will buy us out."[106] Dewitt spoke to the bouncer for a few more minutes, and avoided expulsion from the bar. But just as he was about to rejoin his friends, the bouncer had one last piece of advice: "For your best interest," he quipped, "I would get your friends and leave."[107]

To many residents of Northeastern Pennsylvania, the name Louis DeNaples conjures a shadowy, intimidating image of fear, power, and influence. The mere mention of including him in this book sparked outrage and criticism from friends and family members alike. Yet, DeNaples is, and has been, one of the wealthiest business entrepreneurs in the region. His notoriety—as many in the region know—does not solely stem from his massive personal wealth, but

---

105   Dick Dewitt, interview by Kenny Luck, 6 March 2011.
106   Ibid.
107   Ibid.

also stems from his alleged ties with organized crime.[108] Those who prostrate themselves before DeNaples's aura of unearned respect are almost certainly *NEPATIZED.*

Fear, Inc.

As the owner of more than 100 businesses, a bank, and the $412 million dollar Mount Airy Casino, DeNaples— among other things—is also a philanthropist and a political campaign contributor, who yields unparalleled power and influence.[109] The University of Scranton, for example, a Jesuit university, has praised him, calling DeNaples, "...a person of great humility and deep devotion to family," after DeNaples donated large sums of money to build the 118,000-sq.-ft. "Patrick and Margaret DeNaples Center," located on Mulberry Street in Scranton.[110] In 1978, DeNaples "pleaded no contest to a conspiracy charge of defrauding the government of $525,000 in contracts relating to the cleanup and recovery of the City of Scranton in the aftermath of Hurricane Agnes."[111] DeNaples was fined $10,000, and was placed on probation for three years. In a twist of irony, in the same month—January 2008—as the opening of the "Patrick and Margaret Center" at the University of Scranton, DeNaples' legal troubles would resurface, this time involving perjury charges.

In December 2006, DeNaples won a state casino license to open Mount Airy Casino in the Poconos. Less than two years later, however, on January 30, 2008, DeNaples was

108   Deabill, Eric, "Louis DeNaples Indicted," 30 January 2008.
109   http://www.slots.cd/pennsylvania-supreme-court-investigation-01092008.html
110   http://www.educationforum.ipbhost.com/index.php?showtopic=17110
111   http://en/wikipedia.org/wiki/Louis_DeNaples

charged with four counts of perjury.[112] Prosecutors in Dauphin County alleged that, while under oath, DeNaples lied about his relationships with the Bufalino Crime Family, and reputed mob boss William D'Elia, when testifying before the state's Gaming Control Board.

After years of innuendo and suggestion, a 14-month investigation into DeNaples's alleged ties with organized crime was launched, watched closely by the public and the media. Prosecutors cited DeNaples's attendance at the funeral of D'Elia's mother in 1980, and the wedding of D'Elia's daughter in 1999.[113] But in April 2009, Dauphin County prosecutors dropped all charges against DeNaples and Joseph Sica. As reported by *The Citizen's Voice*, Dauphin County District Attorney Edward Marsico said that he had "achieved his goal in seeing DeNaples leave the gambling business."[114]

MEMORABLE MOMENTS

In 2006, DeNaples told investigators that he could not identify former Philadelphia Mayor John Street in a photograph because he thought that "all black people look alike." DeNaples later apologized, saying, "I want to apologize for the insensitivity of this remark. It was wrong, I shouldn't have said it, and I am sorry that I did."

---

112   "Louis DeNaples and Mount Airy Casino Timeline," The Associated Press, 14 April 2009.
113   http://mafianewstoday.com/tag/louis-denaples/
114   Swift, Robert and Dave Janoski, "DeNaples, Sica Charges Dropped," The Citizen's Voice, 15 April 2009.

The Pennsylvania Gaming Control Board, among other things, ruled that DeNaples "cannot profit from casino revenues nor receive compensation." In addition, Mount Airy is now owned by Lisa DeNaples, Louis DeNaples' daughter. Finally, since the charges have been dropped, Louis DeNaples, the family patriarch, filed a lawsuit in an attempt to "regain his seat on the board of directors of First National Community Bank."[115] On the board of directors for more than 35 years, DeNaples's efforts have failed, and it is not clear where the matter stands at present.

Sica Claus

Mark Guydish—a *Times Leader* reporter—recalled in a January 2008 article titled, "The Damning Indictment of a Local Priest," a "Breakfast with Santa" he attended at St. Aloysius Elementary School in Wilkes-Barre weeks before the article was published. But Santa Claus looked familiar. As it turned out, Santa would be indicted one month later. "The man donning the Santa beard" Guydish wrote, "was Sica."[116] At the time, Sica was St. Aloysius' assistant pastor.[117] "Having a priest play Santa for kids," Guydish continued, "would be the ideal melding of secular and religious, and could produce plenty of teaching moments, especially for older children who might be onto the trick."[118]

Sica's appearance as Santa at St. Aloysius in December 2007 is comical. One wonders if he whispered his now infamous line to the children, murmured weeks later to threat-

---

115   McDonald, Joe, "Louis DeNaples' Attempt to Regain Bank Seat Thwarted," The Times-Tribune, 6 February 2010.
116   Guydish, Mark, "The Damning Indictment of a Local Priest," The Times Leader, 2 January 2008.
117   Ibid.
118   Ibid.

en an arresting police officer: "I bet I can find out stuff about you."[119] If Sica has any of the omniscience the *real* Santa is supposed to have, than it's certain he can "find out stuff." (This was not the beginning of Sica's acting career. According to Chris Kelly of the *Times-Tribune*, Sica "played himself on the funny, but ill-fated sitcom *Life with Bonny*. The show was cancelled in 2004 after two seasons.")

Sica—a long-time friend and cohort of DeNaples—gained the attention of the media in January 2008, when he was arrested and charged with one count of perjury. In an interview, Sica recalled the day of his arrest. "They came to arrest me that morning, and they took me to Dunmore's police barracks," Sica said. "Then [I was] off to central court. They took me to Dauphin County to stand before Judge Hoover."[120]

At the time of the arrest, Sica was chaplain of Mercy Hospital in Scranton and, as reported by *The Morning Call*, he had "amassed debts of $218,000" while his salary was a mere $880 a month.[121] What is more, Sica seemed to have a history of financial troubles. In 1997, for instance, he declared bankruptcy—but as First Assistant District Attorney Francis Chardo made clear in a January 2008 news report—Sica owned a 2007 jeep that was paid for.[122] Also, the $218,000 debt he owed at the time of his arrest was owed to the First National Community Bank, an institution owed by Louis DeNaples.

---

119   Mcauliffe, Josh, "The Rev. Joseph Sica Writes a new Book on Value of Forgiveness in Wake of Legal Troubles," The Times-Tribune, 8 December 2009.
120   Joesph Sica, interview by Kenny Luck, 9 March 2010.
121   Birkbeck, Matt, "DeNaples' Priest Had Deep Debt," The Morning Call, 4 January 2008.
122   Birkbeck, Matt and Christina Gostomski, "DeNaples' Priest Arrested," The Morning Call, 3 January 2008.

During the interview, Sica did not revisit the curious paraphernalia found on him at the time of the arrest. As it is now widely known, Sica was carrying a hand gun and $1000 in cash.[123] The media had fun poking at the priest's unusual choice of personal banking and self-protection.

Chardo noted that it struck him as "odd" for a priest to own a hand gun.[124] At any rate, nothing emerged from the gun incident, but it made for good satire, at least for awhile. Everyone seemed to be in on the joke except Sica. "You learn in life that you are always going to have critics, cynics, and detractors, who are going to keep putting it in your face," he explained. "Mafia priest, mob priest, gun-packing priest, a thousand dollars in cash—there are some people who are not going to let you forget what happened."[125]

What happened was a legal ordeal that lasted from January 2008 to April 2009. Initially, the prosecution believed that Sica's testimony was "intentionally false."[126] The priest was accused of lying under oath, when asked about his relationship with noted mob boss Russell Bufalino. According to the prosecution, Sica had written to Bufalino throughout the years, and had maintained a relationship with him and his wife, Carrie Bufalino (excerpts provided below).

In the end, the charges against Sica were dropped and his record was expunged. "I walked away from it feeling no anger, no bitterness, and no revenge," Sica said. "I can't do much about those 14-months, but keep on moving

123   Jackson, Peter, "Priest's Perjury Arrest Linked to PA Casino Probe," The Associated Press, 2 January 2008.
124   Ibid.
125   Joesph Sica, interview by Kenny Luck, 9 March 2010.
126   Mauriello, Tracie, "Priest Accused of Lying about His Mob Ties in Casino Case," Harrisburg Post-Gazette, 3 January 2008.

The following are excerpts from letters written by Sica, which the Court of Common Pleas of Dauphin County used against him in 2008. The court documents noted, "Because of the length and closeness of their friendship, Fr. Sica's relationship to known criminals was material to whether DeNaples had a relationship with the same known criminals." The court documents added, "Based upon the evidence we have obtained and considered, which establishes a prima facie case, we, the members of the Fourth Dauphin County Investigating Grad Jury, recommend that the District Attorney… institute criminal proceedings against Joseph F. Sica and charge him with one count of perjury."

Dear Russ & Carrie—
Words cannot express my thankfulness to both of you! You have done a lot for me and you mean a lot to me.
Rest assured of my continued love and prayers.
Love Joe

Dear Russ—
…I will not give up, because I want you to have peace and freedom along with justice, all of which you deserve. Hope all is well with you. Billy's back yard looks great. The children really enjoyed Christmas in July at Camp Saint Andrew. I have Santa Claus flown in by helicopter.
Well take care and don't work too hard, keep fighting. My love to Carrie.
Love Joe

Dear Mrs. Thornburgh (former Governor Dick Thornburg's wife),
I am a priest living in Williamsport. I am writing to you on behalf of my friend Mr. Russell Bufalino… Recently Russell was sentenced to prison, for a crime he did not commit. Very briefly, Russell was set-up by the federal government… It is all a conspiracy against a man who has lived a life of honesty, generosity, justice, and a belief in the American system…
Russell is a perfect example of a conspiracy, so what I am asking is for you to help me in giving Russell the freedom and justice he deserves. In helping Russell, you are taking a stand against injustice and immoral measures used in our government…
Sincerely yours,
Joseph Sica

forward."[127] Months after the charges were dropped, Sica published a book titled, *Forgiveness: One Step at a Time.* For Sica, the book was a catharsis. "I was writing this book during all of that, so forgiveness was an important topic for me," he said.[128]

Casino Marino

It is easy to imagine the DeNaples legal saga as a poorly produced, made-for-television movie, complete with corrupt priests, gun-packing mobsters, and enormous sums of money. One essential element that is missing in the cast of characters, however, is the hard-cutting politician. Luckily, one does not need to look very far: Enter Republican Congressman Tom Marino of Pennsylvania's 10th Congressional District.

Marino beat two-term Democrat Chris Carney in the 2010 midterm elections, opening the way for more dubious dealings, a questionable relationship with DeNaples, and a radical conservative agenda. (During a February 2011 visit to King's College, Marino identified himself as a member of the Tea Party, and called the group, "A quintessential example of American democracy.") A resident of Cogan Station, PA, Marino served as the Lycoming County district attorney from 1992 to 2002. He later went to work as an in-house attorney for DeNaples, earning $250,000 a year before going to Washington.[129]

Throughout the election, Carney's campaign tried their best to link Marino with DeNaples, calling him "a

---

127   Joesph Sica, interview by Kenny Luck, 9 March 2010.
128   Ibid.
129   Birkbeck, Matt, "Rep. Carney: Show Me the Letter," <u>The Morning Call,</u> 1 September 2010.

flawed candidate whose values are out of step with the 10th District."[130] More importantly, however, Marino was caught in a series of questionable incidents which, surprisingly, did little to tarnish his bid for congress. In April 2010, for instance, he misreported his earnings. On Marino's 2009 financial disclosure statement, he "reported that he had earned $24,999 working for DeNaples," when the real figure was $249,999.[131] "It was really a typing error," said Jason Fitzpatrick, Marino's spokesman, "and [it] will be amended and corrected."[132] Nevertheless, there were other unexplained consistencies. While working as U.S. Attorney for the Middle District of Pennsylvania in 2007, "Marino was probed by the Justice Department's Office of Professional Responsibility for allegedly violating several department guidelines."[133] As noted above, Marino then resigned, and went to work for—you guessed it—Louis DeNaples. But Marino claims there was never an investigation. "I would certainly be one of the first ones to know," he said.[134] Yet, the Justice Department's Office of Professional Responsibility told another story.

According to sources, the trouble began in 2005, when Marino had "provided a reference on DeNaples' gaming application for Mount Airy Casino and Resort, even as Marino's office was investigating DeNaples."[135] Moreover, once this information became public, it developed into a

---

130   http://hosted.ap.org/dynaic/external/pre-election/bios
131   Birkbeck, Matt, "GOP Congressman Candidate Thomas Marino Misreported Income," The Morning Call, 13 April 2010.
132   Ibid
133   Birkbeck, Matt, "Marino Resigned While Under Review," The Morning Call, 1 October 2010.
134   Krawczeniuk, Borys, "Marino: No More DeNaples Questions," The Times-Tribune, 19 October 2010.
135   Birkbeck, Matt, "GOP Congressman Candidate Thomas Marino Misreported Income," The Morning Call, 13 April 2010.

public relations problem for Marino. At first, when asked about the referral letter in April 2010, Marino said that his superiors thought that it was "nothing at of the ordinary."[136] But then, when Marino was asked about the letter again months later, he claimed he "didn't need approval to give DeNaples a reference."[137]

As the election approached, and with pressure from the Democrats, the congressional candidate decided not to address the issue. In mid-October, Marino told the *Times-Tribune* that he "didn't want to take any more questions on a controversy."[138] As reported by *Mother Jones*, "Deborah Rhode, a legal ethics expert at Stanford University Law School, said '[Marino's reference letter] suggests that there is a relationship that may be compromised by a conflict of interest'."[139] In the end, despite his dubious dealings, Marino was elected, and at present represents Pennsylvania's 10th District. It is not clear to what extent his relationship with DeNaples will affect his career in politics.

Would the Real DeNaples Please Stand Up?

Louis DeNaples, the patriarch of one of Pennsylvania's most well-known and notorious families, is a man shrouded in mystery. For more than three decades, DeNaples has built a personal fortune, while oscillating in and out of the public's attention. Although no one has been able to prove it, innuendo and suggestion that DeNaples is associated

---

136   Krawczeniuk, Borys, "Marino Contradicts in DaNaples Discussion," The Times-Tribune, 29 September 2010.
137   Birkbeck, Matt, "Marino Changes Story," The Morning Call, 28 September 2010.
138   Baumann, Nick, "Tom Marino's Free Pass," Mother Jones, 29 October 2010.
139   Ibid.

with organized crime continues to this day.

As illustrated by the 14-month perjury investigation, the public's insatiable thirst for drama and controversy in Northeastern Pennsylvania remains unquenched, and DeNaples has stepped in to meet the demand. It becomes difficult to distinguish fact from fiction, truth from falsity, when dealing with such a reclusive individual. And many residents of the region seem not to care: They seem only to become more spellbound by the DeNaples aura with each passing generation and decade. Finally, it is important to remember that, no matter how much his wealth, power, and mystery, beneath the veneer of fear and intimidation, DeNaples is just an elderly man, who at times in his life has cultivated an image even he cannot sustain. That may be the simplest truth to accept. But people tend to indulge in fantasies, for they may be easier to grasp than reality.

five

Time for Tea

"No matter what government office you are in, we are watching, and we are coming for you!"
—**Jim Billman**, *Gun Carrying Tea Party Activist*

When speaker Jim Bridge took to the stage at a Tea Party rally in Bloomsburg, PA, in April 2010, he adjusted the microphone, leaned forward, and asked the crowd: "Are you hanging onto your guns and Bibles?" It is a scene common at many Tea Party rallies: Discontented conservatives voicing their opposition to a government they perceive as intrusive and corrupt. Many Tea Partiers have gained national attention in recent months, due largely to violence at rallies, alleged racist undertones, and aggressive rhetoric.

Bridge is the lead spokesman for the Recall NJ Movement, a grassroots organization similar to the Tea Party. His question to the audience was followed by a long, passionate speech in which he attacked everything from immigrants and the media, to liberals and the "Obama Regime." Among the speakers at the rally were Pennsylvania gubernatorial candidate Sam Rohrer, Patrick Henry played by Michael Harrison, and former Hazleton Mayor Lou Barletta.

Having formed in early 2009 as a conservative response to the Obama Administration, the Tea Party, and other self-proclaimed "patriot" groups, tend to engage in paranoid, conspiratorial rhetoric—sometimes against reality. With independent groups springing up in Scranton, Wilkes-Barre, Bloomsburg, and Stroudsburg, the Tea Party Movement is well entrenched in Pennsylvania.

"We've accomplished recognition," said Norman Wahner, co-founder of the NEPA Tea Party, after being asked about the reception of the movement. "We've been recognized by the opposition, Republicans and Democrats."[140] Wahner formed the NEPA Tea Party last year because he believes it is something "people have been looking for." Originally from New Jersey, Wahner has always had a "passion for politics," and says that the Tea Party will remain unaffiliated with any political party.

"Our central message is that we are not a political party," he explained. "I have no time for the Republicans or the Democrats. If we don't remain independent, we are dead. This has got to stay grassroots."[141]

In an interview, Professor Terry Madonna called the Tea Party "a force to be reckoned with." As the Director of the Franklin and Marshall College Poll, Madonna, speaking in April 2010, believed that the Tea Party movement would impact the upcoming November 2010 elections. "Who the candidates are, what elections we are talking about, and whether the Tea Party activists are motivated on behalf of a candidate or not," he explained, noting the factors that could influence the elections. "Geographically, my sense is that it is stronger in the south-central parts of Pennsylva-

---

140   Norman Wahner, interview by Kenny Luck, 28 March 2010.
141   Ibid.

nia, and in the southwest, than it is in the cities."[142]

With a rampant blue-collar demographic and largely rural landscape, Northeastern Pennsylvania seems to be the perfect region for Tea Party activities, as demonstrated by several rallies already held throughout the region. But it is important to point out the obvious hypocrisy of the Tea Partiers. Fanatical and uncompromising, they do not consistently apply the anti-government sentiment to *all* government *all* of the time. Contrary to many of their beliefs, the Tea Party is largely a right-wing movement.

Right-wing Rage

Today's Tea Partiers are the ideological heirs of people like John C. Calhoun and Daniel Shays—not of the Founding Fathers as they claim. In Massachusetts, after hefty taxes were levied to help pay off Revolutionary War debt, Shays organized a group of farmers to violently oppose the measure. The uprising was put down, but a few years later in Pennsylvania, "The Whiskey Rebellion" erupted following a similar tax initiative. Once again, government troops were sent to subdue the revolt.

In the years before the Civil War, South Carolina Congressmen John C. Calhoun argued that states should "nullify" any federal law that conflicted with state law. This audacious claim has been echoed by Republican Texas Governor Rick Perry who, after hearing about President Obama's Health Care proposal in 2009, advocated that Texas should withdraw from the United States, and establish itself as an independent republic.[143] Apart from undermining the

---

142   G. Terry Madonna, interview by Kenny Luck, 13 April 2010.
143   <http://www.huffingtonpost.com/2009/04/15/gov-rick-perry-texas-coul_n_187490.html>

idea of a federal government, Calhoun's treatise on nulli-
fication was in part used as the philosophical justification
for the Southern Confederacy, and is being used now by
Tea Party activists.

If one were to attend anti-war peace rallies in 2004, he
or she would probably hear uncomplimentary things said
about former President George W. Bush. The inflammatory
rhetoric on the left, however, is highly differentiated from
what is happening at present with the Tea Party. American
liberal anti-government sentiment can be traced back to
Henry David Thoreau who, in 1865, was put in jail because
he refused to pay a poll tax that supported the Mexican War
and slavery—two things he thought immoral. Traditional
conservatism insists on preserving institutions and incre-
mental change. The style of conservatism endorsed by the
Tea Party, by contrast, is far more reactionary. In addition,
it is instructive to remember how not a single utterance
emerged about the inflating federal bureaucracy during the
Bush years from these same groups who now, during the
Obama presidency, see the federal government as an intrusive monolith.

> "The Tea Party are crazy people who, just like in
> a banana republic, run to the hills to continue
> the fight. They don't understand that they are
> a minority, that they lost the election, and that
> most people don't think like that. They then be-
> come outraged when they find this to be true.
> They don't understand that a majority of the
> American public do not think like them.'"
> —*Duke Barrett*

Consider Wayne Risch, member of both Luzerne County Campaign for Liberty and the Tea Party. "I am in favor of any policies that are going to give personal freedom back to individuals," Risch said. "We are all individual sovereigns. The federal government has been encroaching on the state's rights for so long and it is time we get the federal government's strangling hands from around the neck of the states."[144] Whether Risch realizes it or not, he is parroting the same rhetoric used by Calhoun, a historical counterpart. When asked what specific rights he believes the federal government has been "encroaching on," he remained silent, but later commented: "There are so many. I wouldn't know where to begin."

In short, there is not much of a difference between the anti-federalists of the past and the anti-tax Tea Parties of today. People like Risch mistakenly cite the Founding Fathers as their influence, but a sober analysis of the matter reveals a different insight: The Tea Party has more in common with Daniel Shays than George Washington. Many Tea Party members insist that they are a non-partisan, independent grass-roots movement that welcomes everyone. "All our members are made up of Democrats, Independents, Republicans," said Wahner. "These people are there to represent themselves, their kids and their grandchildren. People are cross-section. We've got different, races, nationalities, and religions."[145] On the surface, this seems true. For example, news commentator Steve Corbett, who describes his politics as "predominantly left-wing," supports the Tea Party. "I support what the Tea Party is doing in terms of holding government accountable, challenging authority,

---

144   Wayne Risch, interview by Kenny Luck, 10 April 2010.
145   Norman Wanher, interview by Kenny Luck, 28 March 2010.

and taking it to whoever [sic] needs it to be taken to," Corbett explained. "What I am supporting is their right to believe in whatever the hell they want to believe in—even if it's wrong! We have that right in the United States."[146]

Yet, as a self-proclaimed liberal, Corbett's belief about the Tea Party seems to go against reality, as statistics tell another story. According to Madonna, despite the all-inclusive rhetoric, the Tea Party is predominantly a Republican, conservative movement. "In our March 2010 Poll, we asked voters in this state what they thought of the Tea Party, and overwhelmingly a majority of Republicans indicated that they are sympathetic with their views," he said. "Sixty percent of Republicans essentially supported the overall direction in which the Tea Party wanted to take the country. So, the overall conclusion that you reach is that Tea Party activists are more likely to be Republican than Democrat, with a mixture of Libertarians thrown in."[147] When asked if it was possible for a liberal like Corbett to support the Tea Party, against his earlier all-inclusiveness, Wahner disagreed. "It doesn't seem to make sense that a staunch liberal would want to be a Tea Party member," Wahner explained, while contradicting his earlier comments, "unless it is their goal to be destructive and tear us down. There's no way that someone that far on the left would announce it, to my mind. And there is no way that they're going to agree about smaller government and the Constitution."[148]

Renita Fennick, Executive Director of the Luzerne County Republican Party, does not see much of a difference between the GOP and the Tea Party movement, either.

146   Steve Corbett, interview by Kenny Luck, 10 April 2010.
147   G. Terry Madonna, interview by Kenny Luck, 13 April 2010.
148   Norman Wanher, interview by Kenny Luck, 28 March 2010.

"I don't know where the differences are. I think that they are almost identical," she said. "I think that, both the Republican Party and the Tea Party organizers are just aghast at what's going on with our liberties right now. I know that the Tea Party likes to remain non-partisan, but I would say that almost all of our ideals, beliefs and goals are pretty much the same. I can't speak for the whole party, but I would say that most Republicans are probably appreciative of the Tea Party and are respectful of the movement. The people are Constitutionalists. They're for liberties, all of the principles of the Republican Party."[149]

Yet if Finnick is forced to find a difference, it would be not so much in principle or ideology, but in form and function. "The Republican Party is an organization, and when our state committee got together to endorse Tom Corbett for Governor and Pat Toomey for Senate, we all followed suit."[150] The Tea Party, on the other hand, is a movement with no hierarchy or clear leadership.

As he discussed the question of the Tea Party's relevance, Madonna suggested that the Tea Party's lack of leadership is illustrative of a movement which shuns authority. "It is kind of fascinating because they seem to shun a leader," he explained. "It's like, no one wants to step forward and be a leader. Some people have spoken at some of these rallies. I know Tom Corbett has been at least to one."[151] Corbett, who is now governor of Pennsylvania, did attempt to appeal to Tea Party sympathies throughout the 2010 general election, as did Senator Rand Paul of Kentucky.

---

149   Renita Finnick, interview by Kenny Luck, 8 April 2010.
150   Ibid.
151   G. Terry Madonna, interview by Kenny Luck, 13 April 2010.

Coffee or Tea?

As she peered out from her eighth story office window in the middle of the afternoon, Lackawanna County Recorder of Deeds Evie Rafalko McNulty noticed a Tea Party rally taking place on Scranton's public square in early 2009.

While noting the odd timing of the event, McNulty wondered: "How come you are not working? Are you laid off? Are you on disability? Are you retired? If that is the case, somewhere along the line the government is helping you."[152]

The Components of Tea Party Ideology

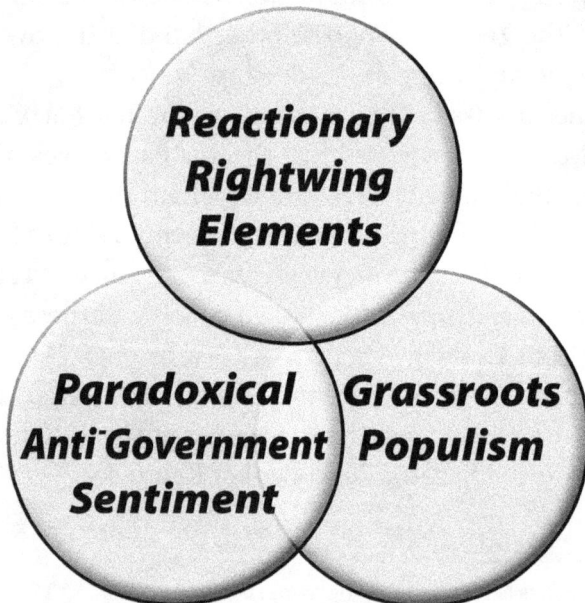

Reactionary Rightwing Elements

Paradoxical Anti-Government Sentiment

Grassroots Populism

---

152   Evie Rafalko McNulty, interview by Kenny Luck, 1 April 2010.

As demonstrated at many rallies, the Tea Party may be on the outer limit of the ideological continuum. Their stated beliefs and oratory are conspiracy-laden, peppered with paranoia, and outright paradoxical. Many have taken notice of the Tea Party hypocrisy. "It's a joke," said Kevin Lynn, when asked what he thought about the Tea Party. "They are not worried about freedom. The only thing that they are worried about is taxes. But where were they for the Iraq War? We spent two and a half billion dollars a week off the books that our grandchildren are going to have to pay for—the very thing that the Tea Party people are complaining about. It was all there in the news, and they were either asleep or in church. But when do they wait to complain? They waited to complain when there was health care that is going to help all of us, and until we had a brown-skinned president. What a coincidence."[153]

There are others who share Lynn's discontent. In January 2010, a Tea Party liberal counterpart movement, the Coffee Party, formed as an alternative grassroots outlet for progressives. It was founded by documentary filmmakers and political activists Annabel Park and Eric Byler who—according to *The New York Times*—were "fed up with government gridlock, but put off by the flavor of the Tea Party."[154] Relying on social networking sites the group has grown exponentially in the past five months and has more than 212,000 members on its Facebook page (as of May 2010). There are Coffee Party chapters in York and Pittsburgh, but none so far in the Scranton/Wilkes-Barre area—yet. On March 27, 2010, a Coffee Party summit was held at Northern Light Espresso Bar in Scranton, right across

---

153   Kevin Lynn, interview by Kenny Luck, 28 April 2010.
154   <http://www.nytimes.com/2010/03/02/us/politics/02coffee.html>

from the Lackawanna County Courthouse where several Tea Party demonstrations had already taken place.

Others, such as Duke Barrett, see the Tea Party for what it is: A conservative movement that can function from the outside throwing stones, but not as an efficient governing entity. Barrett thinks that the Tea Party activists are a lot of the same people who voted for George Bush and, at that time, had no problem supporting the government. "A lot of these Tea Party people are the same anti-immigration people," Barrett said. "They're the conservative base who wants the GOP to be even more conservative. And even though 98 percent of the American public under Obama received fairly significant tax cuts, and even though Republicans ran up 93 percent of the current deficit, these are people who, for whatever reason, have a picture in their head of what they wish America to be, and the facts be damned."[155]

We Are Coming For You!

To their credit, Tea Party activists do raise several important questions: What are the limits of state power? Whose interests should the government represent? What are the limits of acceptable dissent? By probing these questions, and others, perhaps we could learn more about ourselves and in the course of the questioning, come to a better understanding of the type of society we want to have. Dissent only becomes problematic when, rather than reason, it is based on fear and hysteria. For now, people such as Jim Billman, head of the Berks County Patriots, see themselves as the legitimate fighting force against what they perceive as a corrupt federal government. While standing in the

---

155   Duke Barrett, interview by Kenny Luck, 25 April 2010.

Bloomsburg City Park in April 2010, joined by roughly 150 other Tea Party members, Billman shouts a positive "Yes" to speaker Jim Bridge's opening question about hanging on to guns and Bibles. As Billman displays his handgun, all innuendo vanishes and the message is clear.

"If you run for office and tell me that you stand for property tax elimination I will hold your feet to the fire," Billman said. "You better damn well believe that I am going to be right there in your face, telling everybody I know, as much as I can, what you really stand for. No matter what government office you are in, we are watching, and are coming for you!"[156]

---

156   Jim Billman, interview by Kenny Luck, 10 April 2010.

six

The Coercive Power
of Bishop Martino

"All I know is it was time for him to go."
—**Father Patrick Sullivan**, *Catholic Church, Ministry in*
Labor-Management Relations

For some supports, former Bishop Joseph Martino represents a long-standing ecclesiastical structure, perhaps as old as the Church itself, which emphasizes tradition over change, authority over individual preferences, and a righteous religiosity over modern secularism. Martino is, of course, the former controversial bishop from the Scranton Diocese who emerged as the leading religious antagonist in Northeastern Pennsylvania. This claim can be measured in terms of Martino's public notoriety, hostility toward unionization, and negativism toward homosexuals. The bishop's legacy of authoritarianism and fanaticism continues to haunt Northeastern Pennsylvania.

Martino shocked the public when he announced his resignation in late summer 2009. Although he became Bishop of the Scranton Diocese in 2003, it was not until the beginning of 2008 when a series of controversies erupted, positioning Martino against politicians, the media and, in some cases, ordinary church goers. Although Martino customarily does not grant interviews, an attempt was made to contact him for this book. However, as happened to others before, the request was denied. "Bishop Martino maintains a policy of no interviews," wrote Heather Betts in an email, an office worker at the Diocese of Scranton. "While he was grateful to receive your kind request, this policy remains in effect."[157]

An Anything-Goes Mindset

When Keith Boykin, a best-selling author and television commentator, was asked to speak at Misericordia University in February 2009 as part of a Black History month presentation, Martino expressed "absolute disapproval"[158] of Boykin's appearance because he is gay. Martino claimed to be upholding Catholic teaching, which traditionally opposes homosexuality. What began as an argument over the speaker's appearance soon turned into a raging debate— via the media—over the nature and scope of tolerance.

Martino opposed Boykin's appearance "not because of his sexual orientation, but because he is a well-known proponent of morality that is disturbingly opposed to Catholic teaching, such as homosexual relations and same-sex marriage."[159] Fair enough. But it is hard not to think that Martino's position is somewhat hypocritical considering

157   Heather Betts, "Request for interview with Bishop Martino," 20 April 2010, personal e-mail (20 April 2010).
158   Sarah Hofius Hall, "Bishop Martino Rips College for Gay-Rights Speaker," *The Times-Tribune,* 17 February 2009.
159   Sarah Hofius Hall, "Bishop Martino Says 'Tolerance' Has Limits," *The Times- Tribune,* 4 March 2009.

the Church itself, the same institution that publically opposes homosexuality, was involved in covering up Church-related controversies and crimes involving homosexuality and pedophilia in recent years.[160]

As the debate continued, Martino's authoritarianism became more apparent. The Scranton Diocese released a statement. In it, Martino argued that there is a difference between "authentic tolerance" and an "anything-goes mindset." The statement was murky, and did not clearly define the meaning of Martino's message. It also contained a contradiction: In one sentence Martino admits that he is not rejecting Boykin because he is gay, but in the next breath rationalizes his opposition because he thinks that the author's lifestyle promotes immorality. Aren't they the same thing? Claiming that his bigotry was divinely inspired, the bishop nevertheless continued his paranoid crusade against Boykin and homosexuality.

The Martino Monologues

In the same month as Boykin's appearance at Misericordia University, Martino opened another battle front. As an employee at a local Catholic elementary school, director and actress Dawn Winarski did not know that her participation in an upcoming production of *The Vagina Monologues* would gain the bishop's attention.

---

160   An internal church document that was publically released in 2002 seems to indicate that the Vatican was aware of many of its pedophile priests. Dated May 29, 1999, "...the order signed by Pope John Paul calls for the defrocking of Robert Burns, a priest who had pled guilty to indecent assault of a child." As far as we know at least 3 Popes were involved in the cover-ups dating back to 1962. What is more, in early 2010 new evidence emerged that Pope Benedict allegedly was involved in a cover-up concerning priests who abused children. To date, the issue has not been resolved. See Russ Kick, *100 Things You're Not Supposed to Know.* (New York: MJF Books, 2004), 241.

Days before the play, Winarski's photo appeared in a local paper. A student who attended an area Catholic high school was also in the photo, along with the rest of the cast. "We were informed at one of the last dress rehearsals that the girl had to leave the show because they threatened to expel her," Winarski recalled. "I thought, 'Oh, my God. That is horrible.' The next day, at our final dress rehearsal, I got called into the office. The principal closed the door and I thought, 'This seems really weird.' She had explained to me that the picture had come across one of the offices at the Scranton Diocese."[161]

Actress Kim Schuetrum recalled the McCarthy-era tactics used by Martino and his acolytes. She said that the cast recognized what was happening to their director. "Two or three days prior to the performance she was notified by her employer, a local Catholic school, that if she did not pull her name from the project completely she would face 'dire consequences' when she came into work Monday morning," Schuetrum said. "As a performer, it is very important to have your director available to you, particularly on the night of the performance. Not having that support there really had an effect on some of the other performers."[162]

Winarski maintains that the Diocese's motivation for keeping her out of the play was not clear. "I said to them at the time, 'But it raises money to fight against violence against women!' I couldn't just put together how that was a bad thing," She explained. "It felt like they were trying to tell me that what I was doing was wrong. How is that wrong when you are helping people? But they said that it was unacceptable. They said that it was inappropriate for

161   Dawn Winarski, interview by Kenny Luck, 10 May 2010.
162   Kim Schetrum, interview by Kenny Luck, 12 May 2010.

someone who worked at a Catholic school to be in it. The Diocese was giving a veiled threat that something very bad would happen if I stayed with the production."[163]

With her livelihood on the line, and against her intuition, Winarski chose not to participate in the play. The pressure from the Diocese was too much. And after all of her hard work, Winarski had to stand by as the show went on. Schuetrum, on the other hand, did perform. As she and other actresses left the building after the show one evening, an unexpected scene was waiting outside. "When we came out of the performance that evening many of us had flyers left on our cars that stated *The Vagina Monologues* forced women to perform; that domestic violence was not committed by men—it was committed by angry lesbians; and that women were being forced to have abortions due to this show," said Schuetrum. "There isn't even a mention of abortion in the show. The flyers had pictures of partially aborted fetuses, which really upset some of the performers. I was incredibly angry because there were a lot of people in our audience that night who were survivors of domestic violence, and they had to come out and find that on their car?"[164]

Although she cannot prove it, Schuetrum believes that church officials were behind the flyers. "There was never hard evidence to prove it," she said, "but if you look at all of the circumstantial evidence, it all kind of points back to [Martino]." Both Winarski and Schuetrum performed in *The Vagina Monologues* the following year. By that time Martino had already retired and, quite predictably, no threats emerged. Yet, the damage from the previous year

163   Dawn Winarski, interview by Kenny Luck, 10 May 2010.
164   Kim Schuetrum, interview by Kenny Luck, 12 May 2010.

had already been done. "I never found myself particularly religious, but what little kind of connection or faith I might have had was completely destroyed after that," Winarski said.[165]

Milz vs. Martino

In June 2008, Michael Milz, President of the Scranton Diocese Association of Catholic Teachers (SDACT), was terminated from his teaching position. The SDACT, which represented union members for more than 30 years, had been seeking recognition by the Scranton Diocese—a proposition Martino repeatedly refused. "Unlike other employees in other occupations, people who work for a religious employer are not covered by the prevailing federal and state labor laws," Milz said.[166] When Martino became bishop, Milz attempted to begin a dialogue with him. That,

MEMORABLE MOMENTS

In February 2009, Martino accused Senator Bob Casey of "cooperating with evil" because Casey refused to back legislation that would block U.S. tax dollars from going to foreign family planning groups. One month later, Martino ordered that if a politician was pro-choice he or she could not receive the Eucharist in the Scranton Diocese. Just before his retirement later that year, Martino was waging a battle with pro-choice politicians and secularism.

---

165   Dawn Winarski, interview by Kenny Luck, 10 May 2010.
166   Michael Milz, interview by Kenny Luck, 20 May 2010.

however, did not occur. "He's never met with us," Milz said. "He was the fourth bishop that we worked under and in every case whenever a new bishop came in I sent him a letter, told him who we were, told him about the organization, and asked to meet with him. We met with them all. We met with O'Conner. We met with Timlin. Martino was somebody who never wanted any kind of dialogue. It was his way or no way, and that was very disconcerting."[167]

Martino later argued that, despite their attempts to talk in private, Milz and the union were selfish and wrong for wanting to organize. "This association's leaders have reasons based on self-interest for wanting to retain their role in some of our schools," Martino wrote in a public letter. "I have been disappointed by the invective and disrespect that have been unleashed against me through public statements and quotes in the media." In a paradoxical fashion, Martino refused to meet with the union members in private, but then blamed them for expressing discontent in public. The bishop said that the union's opposition to him was disrespectful, and like something out of the McCarthy-era, he would not let such "disrespect" stand. [168] Milz was laid off by the diocese. "I got fired for my union activities," Milz explained. "They set it up to appear that there was some other reason for losing my job after 34 years of teaching. Without any legal evidence to pursue it, there was nothing that I could do."[169]

Months later, in another blow to the rights of the workers, the Vatican affirmed Martino's decision not to recog-

167   Michael Milz, interview by Kenny Luck, 20 May 2010.
168   < http://thecatholicwatchdog.wordpress.com/2008/02/21/a-message-from-bishop-martino/>
169   Michael Milz, interview by Kenny Luck, 20 May 2010.

nize SDACT.[170] This decision seemed contradictorily because the United States Conference of Catholic Bishops
named the Dignity of Work and the Rights of Workers as
one of the seven key themes of Catholic Social Teaching.[171]
Milz was also disappointed by the Vatican's decision because "the Catholic Church has always been a strong proponent of the right to organize."[172] The Vatican's support of
Martino's hard stance was appalling to some, and invited
criticism in the press. "We kept up a steady drumbeat of
criticism against the decision made by the diocese, particularly blaming Bishop Martino because obviously in a
Catholic diocese the bishop's word is law," said Milz.[173]

Although Martino was now operating under direct approval from the Vatican, not everyone submitted to the intimidation. The Rev. Patrick J. Sullivan, an activist of the
Catholic Church's Ministry in Labor-Management Relations for more than 30 years[174] and a professor at King's
College, took a public stand against the bishop. In a February 2008 letter, Sullivan claimed that his attempts to talk
to Martino had only been met with "silence or refusal."[175]
"First of all, I wrote him a personal private letter and never
received an answer," Sullivan recalled. "I had been working
with labor groups for eight years."[176] Sullivan argued that
the bishop's actions toward the union were "a violation of
church teaching," and when his requests were ignored, Sullivan then decided to go public. "He really couldn't answer

170   <http://www.religiondispatches.org/blog/humanrights/632/>
171   Ibid.
172   Michael Milz, interview by Kenny Luck, 20 May 2010.
173   Michael Milz, interview by Kenny Luck, 20 may 2010.
174   <http://www.democraticunderground.com/discuss/duboard.
php?az=view_all&address=367x8041>
175   Ibid.
176   Patrick Sullivan, interview by Kenny Luck, 3 May 2010.

my challenges in light of Catholic Social Teaching."[177]

Martino, on the other hand, decided to skip over Sullivan's challenge all together, charging that the union leaders concerns were "misleading, inaccurate, or simply false."[178] Sullivan contested that claim, making clear that "the proof of such an outlandish charge beggars, unless the records of negation sessions and financial details are presented to the public." Sullivan added: "Otherwise, an unjust accusation is made about the teachers."[179]

In the light of Sullivan's rebuttal letter, Martino never produced reliable evidence for his claim. The bishop seemed to meet his match. "We were the first people that he really took on in the way that he did," Milz said, commenting on his and Sullivan's efforts.

"I think it probably threw him that we didn't just say, 'Oh yeah! Screw us over. bishop. We don't care. We are going to just walk away.' I think he was shocked, not only from us, but from the vast majority of the public that saw what he did to us was wrong. From there, every time he did something equally as nasty he got the same kind of criticism."[180] Moreover, when asked how he would interpret Martino's silence toward his letter, Sullivan added, "He wasn't interested in responding to me because he had no argument."[181]

After a two year battle, Monsignor Joseph Bambera, who would later replace Martino, sat down to talk in September 2009. According to Milz, it was the "first commu-

---

177   Ibid.
178   < http://thecatholicwatchdog.wordpress.com/2008/02/21/a-message-from-bishop-martino/>
179   < http://www.democraticunderground.com/discuss/duboard.php?az=view_all&address=367x804>
180   Michael Milz, interview by Kenny Luck, 20 may 2010.
181   Patrick Sullivan, interview by Kenny Luck, 3 May 2010.

The Elements of Martinian Authoritarianism

- In February 2009, Martino threatened to fire two diocese employees and one Catholic high school student if they were associated with the local production of *The Vagina Monologues*—a production which "raises awareness and funding for women's shelters and battered women."

- In that same month, Martino publically threatened to close St. Peter's Cathedral in Scranton if several Irish American groups featured pro-choice politicians at any of their annual events.

- Throughout his tenure as bishop, Martino closed about 30 high schools and announced in January 2009 that "the Diocese of Scranton would close or consolidate half of its 209 parishes."

- When Keith Boykin, a homosexual, best-selling author and former Clinton Administration aide spoke at Misericordia University for a Black History Month event, Martino expressed "absolute disapproval." What is more, Martino then publically refused to meet with the universities in private, and called upon the diocese's four universities to prove their Catholic identity by submitting the course syllabi of religious related classes. The situation was reminiscent of McCarthy-era tactics used by paranoid, right-wing politicians in the early 1950s.

- In October 2008, during a parish forum on "Faithful Citizenship" hosted in Honesdale, PA, Martino unexpectedly showed up and announced that, "No United States Conference of Catholic Bishops document is relevant in this diocese." Furthering adding that, "There is one teacher in this diocese, and these points are not debatable."

- In a well-known move, Martino decertified the Scranton Diocese Association of Catholic Teachers. The union had represented members for more than 30 years, and the decision sparked off litigation and even got the Vatican involved. Marino then replaced the SCACT with a diocesan organization of his approval.

- Martino instructed church workers—lay ministers and priests—not to give Communion to anyone he deemed "unworthy." The move was suspected to be aimed at then vice presidential candidate Joe Biden, who grew-up in Scranton and was a pro-choice Catholic.

nication with the diocese, of any kind."[182] But as months passed, and after Bambera was sworn in as bishop, communication with the diocese broke down once again. "Since he has been bishop I have not received any kind of response from my last two letters," Milz said. "We are waiting to hear from him. Since Martino left last fall, things have been very quiet. We've asked other unions to tone down their criticism of the diocese with the hope that we have a better relationship, but so far we haven't seen that." The way in which Bishop Bambera will respond to, or resolve the requests of the union remains to be seen. "Our patience is starting to grow a little thin. We are denied rights that every other working group in America has."[183]

The Meaning of Martino

On August 31, 2009, after six years as bishop, Martino announced his retirement at age 63—a relatively young age for a bishop to retire.[184] Monsignor Joseph C. Bambera was chosen to replace Martino. Since its founding in 1868, the Scranton Diocese has had ten bishops. Among them, Martino is perhaps the most controversial. Never before has a bishop polarized so many churchgoers, has been so popular in the media, and has invoked such debate. In essence, Martino, whose name has appeared in *The New York Times*, *Time Magazine*, *The Washington Post*, *The Chicago Tribune*, *USA Today*, and *The Associated Press*,[185] was a media figure who epitomized an authoritative religiosity in the Scranton Diocese.

---

182   Sarah Hofius Hall, "New Diocesan Leader Ends Bishop Martino's Stonewall of Teachers Union," *The Times-Tribune*, 14 October 2009.

183   Michael Milz, interview by Kenny Luck, 20 may 2010.

184   The mandatory retirement age for bishops is 75.

185   Laura Legere, "Bishop Takes Place on National Stage," *The Times-Tribune*, 30 November 2008.

One of the great intriguers about Martino is that his rhetoric and actions, if evaluated closely, were guided, and shaped by, a deep philosophical conviction rooted in authoritarianism. His unwillingness to compromise, plus his belief in his own supreme authority and the righteousness of his cause, are, by any standards, a dangerous mix. Many of Martino's followers unquestioningly supported the bishop and his actions, despite the pain and trouble that these actions have caused. Consider John A. Chopyak. In an April 2009 letter to the editor, Chopyak attempted to argue that Martino was a positive force for Catholics. "Thank you, God, for Bishop Martino," he wrote. "The Bishop is a true courageous shepherd of his flock. Every diocese changes with time and its shepherd must mold and guide it according to the almost 2,000 years of bedrock tradition outlining its foundation."[186] Chopyak does not hesitate to identify himself as a member of Martino's "flock"—a sort of unthinking, unreflective collectivity of individuals who hands over all personal autonomy to Church bureaucrats. It is this kind of thinking, Milz argues, that leads to more problems. "I've had a number of people who have been very critical of my role," he said. "You've got people who, if the bishop says this, and if you question the bishop, than you are on the side of evil."[187] The criticisms against Milz were not limited to benign insults: He received death threats. "I've had my life threatened a number of times. I've had my family threatened," he said, while recalling the extreme backlash he faced. "If you do anything in opposition of the Church, or any of the Church representatives, you are going to face

186   John A. Chopyak, "Bishop Martino is a Leader Who Makes Necessary Change," *The Citizen's Voice*, 1 April 2008.
187   Michael Milz, interview by Kenny Luck, 20 May 2010.

criticism."[188] Milz said that the attacks from those who supported Martino did not deter him. When asked what he thought about Martino's legacy, Milz said he was happy the bishop had stepped down. "He was not somebody who should have held that position," he said. "I think most people would agree that he was a misfit. He finally came to that conclusion on his own. I have to give him credit for one thing: He had the sense to get out before he did even more damage. Anybody that can't sit across the table from you, and defend a position that their taking, I see as an absolute weakness. I think the man had emotional, psychological issues that were unresolved. I think that came out throughout the course of his entire tenure. We were the first to feel it, and by far not the last."[189]

When Martino closed the elementary school where she worked in June 2009, Winarski had to find a new job. After the threats she faced before over her involvement in *The Vagina Monologues*, losing her job actually had a positive outcome: It freed her from Martino's coercive power. When asked if she thinks that the Diocese of Scranton is better off since Martino's retirement, Winarski agreed that it was. "I do think it is better off, but I can't say how much will change," she explained. "The new bishop appears to be at least more pleasant. There was just something just not right, in my opinion, about Martino. With everything, he was 'Off with their heads! Off with their heads!' To me, it didn't seem like it was necessarily church teachings as much as it was his own personal vendetta against anything that he felt was not good Christian behavior."[190]

188   Ibid.
189   Ibid.
190   Dawn Winarski, interview by Kenny Luck, 10 May 2010.

The final question worth asking is: How will Martino's past actions, which seemed quite desperate at times, impact the future of the Church? The current evidence suggests that Martino did more harm than good. The Diocese reported that as of early 2009 there were 188 active priests, and the number is estimated to drop to 147 in 2012 and only 122 by 2017.[191] In addition to these dismal numbers, Martino seems to have divided, rather than united, many area Catholics. A Facebook group entitled "Movement to Remove Bishop Martino" had (as of April 2009) nearly 700 members, while a Martino support group had less than half that amount.[192] One can speculate that many Martino supporters are most likely of an older demographic, offering support to the Church for generations. Yet, if young people tend to be at odds with the bishop and what he represents, is it not the next generation that will be the future of the church?

Corrupt Clergymen

Responding to an outcry of molestation accusations, the United States Conference of Bishops gathered to draft the Charter for the Protection of Children and Young People in 2002.[193] The purpose of the charter was to provide "transparency and accountability" for an otherwise shadowy bureaucratic institution.[194] That same year, revelations of sexual misconduct by priests and clergy became public,

---

191   Laura Legere, "Parish Consolidations through 2012 Will Leave Fewer Than 30 Across Lackawanna County," *The Times-Tribune*, 1 February 2009.
192   Erin Moody, "Supporters and Detractors of Bishop Martino Having Their Say on Facebook", *The Citizen's Voice*, 2 April 2009.
193   Roja Heydarpour, "Diocese of Scranton Mum on Sex Abuse Policy Case," *The Times-Tribune*, 13 July 2008.
194   Ibid.

and the new charter was the Church's attempt to defend itself.

The Scranton Diocese, according to a diocesan report, admits that at least 25 of its priests have been "accused of having sexual contact with minors since 1950."[195] With such a long history of criminal activity within the church, it seemed unimaginable that the Scranton Diocese would fail to fully embrace the new charter. But it did. Of the 195 dioceses nationwide, the Scranton Diocese was one of five dioceses that declined to participate in an audit that would reveal how the Diocese of Scranton integrated the suggestions made by The United States Conference of Bishops.[196][197] Church detractors argued in 2008—six years after the charter was enacted—that "the Diocese of Scranton's refusal to discuss specifics of the program [was] evidence of its inadequacy."[198] In essence, under the provisions set forth by the charter, each diocese is responsible for polic-

> **As reported in a 2006 Times Leader article, "As early as the 1960s and as late as 2002, the Scranton Diocese knowingly employed priests who had been accused of sexual misconduct."**

195   http://www.bishop-accountability.org/usccb/natureandscope/dioceses/scrantonpa.htm
196   Roja Heydarpour, "Diocese of Scranton Mum on Sex Abuse Policy Case," *The Times-Tribune*, 13 July 2008.
197   Dave Janoski, "The Sins of our Fathers," *The Times Leader*, 9 July 2006.
198   Roja Heydarpour, "Diocese of Scranton Mum on Sex Abuse Policy Case," *The Times-Tribune*, 13 July 2008.

ing itself, an idea that is utterly ridiculous. Barbra Blaine, president of Survivors Network of Those Abused by Priests (SNAP), commented: "Obviously, no institution can police [itself], and the church has done a horrific job."[199] When an accusation is made against a clergy member a report is made, and "the diocese launches its own investigation." According to a 2008 story by *The Times-Tribune*, "the findings are [then] sent to a review board."[200] The review board consists of five members whom, since 2008, the Scranton Diocese has refused to identify.

Covered-up Crimes and the Rev. Robert Gibson

In 2006, *The Times Leader* launched an involved investigation into the history of abuse and corruption within the Diocese of Scranton. After the review of eight lawsuits and interviews with victims, the paper was able to conclude that three former bishops knew of the crimes and misconduct by clergymen within the diocese. In particular, former Bishop James C. Timlin was, as reported by *The Times Leader*, "personally aware during his administration as bishop from 1984 through 2003 that at least five of his priests had been accused of sexual misconduct with minors."[201] Michael Baumann, for example, was sexually abused by Rev. Robert Gibson in 1973 and 1974. Although Gibson's abuse took place before Timlin's tenure, it demonstrates a historical fact pattern that cannot be ignored. "I think that organization, going back years and years, has covered for these guys," said Baumann, who now lives in Virginia. "Whether it was Caparelli or some of the other

---

199   Ibid.
200   Ibid.
201   Dave Janoski, "The Sins of Our Fathers," *The Times Leader*, 9 July 2006.

Profiles of Pedophile Priests

The Rev. Robert Gibson

Gibson sexually abused Michael Baumann in 1973 and 1974. Gibson's criminal activities would continue into the 1990s before he was finally stripped of his collar.

The Rev. Virgil Bradley Tetherow ("Father Gabriel")

In 2005, Father Gabriel admitted to downloading child pornography from January to December 2004 on his secretary's computer as well as the one in his rectory room.

The Rev. Eric Ensey and the Rev. Carlos Urrutigoity

Ensey and Urrutigoity were priests within the Society of St. John in Pike County. In January 2002, both priests were removed after molestation allegations emerged. A federal judge later order psychological records of the two be turned in to authorities.

Assistant Pastor Robert N. Caparelli

A lawsuit filed in 2005 alleged that Caparelli molested David Irvin in 1969 while Caparelli served as assistant pastor at St. Mary's Church in Old Forge. The Assistant Pastor died in jail in 1994 after pleading guilty to molesting two Pike County altar boys.

Father Albert Liberatore

The same year that David Irvin filed his lawsuit against Caparelli, Father Albert Liberatore, a former University of Scranton professor, was arrested in 2004 in Lackawanna County for allegedly abusing a former altar boy from his parish.

Bishop Emeritus James C. Timlin

Although not a parish priest, nor a pedophile, Timlin was aware that at least five of his priests had been accused of sexual misconduct during his tenure as bishop of the Diocese of Scranton during the years 1984 to 2002.

prolific child rapists they had working there."[202]

Gibson was Baumann's eight-grade religion teacher at Notre Dame Junior/Senior High School in East Strouds-burg.[203] Baumann recalled the threats that Gibson made. "At first, he tried to convince me that my mother knew what he was doing, and that she was all right with it," he said. "Then Gibson threatened my brothers and sisters with either visits of their own, or being expelled from the Catholic school they were attending. Later, he flat-out threatened to kill me."[204] But no action was taken to stop Gibson's abuse. "That did a lot of damage to me," he said. "It has done a lot of damage to my wife. It has done a lot of damage to my relationship with my kids. It has caused a lot of damage to my extended family. There was definitely a change in me when I became the play toy of a Catholic priest."[205]

In 1995, Gibson's pedophilia was again unveiled. According to a newspaper report, the diocese "was approached by an attorney for a man who claimed he had been sexually abused by Gibson 20 years earlier."[206] An admitted criminal, Gibson resigned and was sent to for treatment, but again, that did not stop his abuse. "And I am sure I wasn't his first victim, and I know that I wasn't his last," Baumann said. "I would conservatively estimate that his victims are probably in the three digits. And that is not unusual based on some of the studies that the Catholic Church has done over the years. Once these guys get started, they then use their

---

202   Michael Baumann, interview by Kenny Luck, 16 December 2010.
203   Laura Legere, "Scranton Diocese Come Clean on Abusive Priest," 27 September 2008.
204   Michael Baumann, interview by Kenny Luck, 16 December 2010.
205   Michael Baumann, interview by Kenny Luck, 16 December 2010.
206   Laura Legere, "Scranton Diocese Come Clean on Abusive Priest," 27 September 2008.

positions having access to lots of kids to abuse. Through intimidation and fear, they keep them quiet."[207]

As late as 1997, Gibson was living under supervised care at St. Ignatius Rectory in Kingston, Pennsylvania. In the spring, a mother had complained that the priest was "paying a troubling amount of attention to her son."[208] An internal church investigation revealed that "the priest was likely 'grooming' the boy" for what the church called, "improper activity."[209] A year later, Gibson was sent to another treatment center in Missouri and was barred from having any contact with minors. Baumann describes the center as "a facility that specializes in housing pedophiles."[210]

More than thirty years after Gibson's abuse, Baumann, a reluctant activist, is committed to exposing the crimes and abuses of the institutional hierarchy of the church. "My biggest problem with this whole thing is not so much with Gibson. It's with the Diocese of Scranton. When they found out what he was doing, they did not take decisive action," he said.[211] "I initially thought the diocese would do the right thing, and the more I dealt with them, the more I realized not only were they not going to do the right thing, but institutionally they had been failing to do the right thing for generations."[212]

Baumann operates the blog "Off My Knees: Standing Up for Myself and Other Victims of Sexual Abuse by Clergy."[213] "The reason I started blogging," he said, "was

207   Michael Baumann, interview by Kenny Luck, 16 December 2010.
208   Laura Legere, "Scranton Diocese Come Clean on Abusive Priest," 27 September 2008.
209   Ibid.
210   Michael Baumann, interview by Kenny Luck, 16 December 2010.
211   Michael Baumann, interview by Kenny Luck, 16 December 2010.
212   Ibid.
213   http://michaelbaumann.wordpress.com/

because I caught the diocese in a lie. Bill Genello, who I think is one of the most accomplished liars on the planet, kept saying that Bishop Martino always personally reached out to victims, and I saw the bullshit fly. I've never spoken to Martino. I've never received a letter from Martino."[214] In fact, Baumann wrote an open letter to Martino, and blasted the bishop for his inaction. An excerpt from the letter reads:

> From my vantage point, I see the Diocese of Scranton as a significant player in the policy of excusing and enabling the sex crimes committed by pedophile priests in your curia. I believe that your administration and the administrations of Bishop Timlin and the previous bishops of Scranton buried reports, prevented and delayed reports to civil authorities in order to outlast the statute of limitations. I believe that the bishops acted in a blatantly criminal and arrogant manner to obstruct justice. I have no doubt that victims came to the Diocese and sought help, justice and guidance. I am sure that many feel, as I do, that they were betrayed and violated all over again.[215]

Martino never adequately responded to the letter—a predictable move since the former bishop never addressed criticism by his opponents.

In the end, however, Baumann has no desire to reform the church. To do so, he says, would be a "complete folly." Rather, he would like changes in the laws and legislatures. "I would like to see legislation passed in every state, like they

---

did in California and in Delaware, which allows victims outside the statute of limitations to take action against, not only their attackers, but the people who protected them," he said.[216] "Pedophilia is a crime," he added, "and people who excuse-away the rape of children don't hold a lot of water with me."

Ongoing Abuse and Hypocrisy

The sexual misconduct and abuse within the Diocese of Scranton started more than 50 years ago and continues into the present. Adult men continue to come forth with new allegations of sexual abuse from priests within the Scranton Diocese. According to the John Jay College of Criminal Justice, which published a report titled, *The Nature and The Scope of the Problem of Sexual Abuse of Minors by Catholic Priests and Deacons in the United States* "there [is] a significant difference between genders, with four out of five alleged victims being male."[217]

Late last year, in November 2010, officials in Maryland began investigating the Rev. Neil McLaughlin. With connections to the Scranton Preparatory School, the University of Scranton, and St. Thomas More Church in Lake Ariel, McLaughlin is accused of abusing minors "during his ministry in Scranton."[218] What is more, McLaughlin was "removed from ministry by the Jesuits in 2006, following allegations of misconduct."[219] At the time of this writing, the outcome of McLaughlin's alleged sexual misconduct remains to be seen. However, one question must be asked: How many

---

216   Michael Baumann, interview by Kenny Luck, 16 December 2010.
217   http://www.usccb.org/nrb/johnjaystudy/incident2.pdf
218   Joe McDonald, "Sexual Misconduct Allegations Surface against Former Scranton Jesuit," 1 December 2010.
219   Ibid.

more child-raping priests are going to get caught before the church begins to take this issue seriously?

Knowing of the abuse—as in former Bishop Timlin's case—and failing to act, is evidence of; a mismanaged and corrupt ecclesiastical system. A problem of this scope does not endure for more than 50 years without internal support, as shown by the aforementioned examples.

This should prompt outrage from churchgoers and the public. Rather, many Catholic devotees continue to make excuses for the crimes and cover-ups by Church officials. This is not a matter of a few bad priests "gone bad"; the problem is widespread and endemic. "They haven't reported the abuse historically," said Baumann. "The Church has pretty much protected its own. I have no interest in the Catholic Church whatsoever. It is probably one of the more slippery organizations on the planet."[220]

In early 2010, even the current pope, Joseph Ratzinger, was accused of covering-up sexual misconduct by clergymen in Germany prior to his position as head of the papacy—more evidence of the scope of this problem. But one does not need to look to the Vatican for allegations of sexual misconduct by priests and clergymen. Simply look to 300 Wyoming Avenue, Scranton, Pennsylvania—the epicenter of the Scranton Diocese—to find myriad cases of ongoing sexual misconduct, abuse, and corruption.

---

220   Michael Baumann, interview by Kenny Luck, 16 December 2010.

seven

"Joe From Old Forge"

The typical WILK FM Caller

"I think the callers are by and large center-right. The reason is a lot of them are losers [who] nobody listens to, so they call radio stations so that they will always be on what a lot of people will be listening to, although not necessarily to them."

—**Kevin Lynn,** *former host of* The Morning News with
Nancy and Kevin

W hen Duke Barrett ("Duke from Dallas") moved to Northeastern Pennsylvania, he immediately recognized something peculiar about the region. "It seemed to me, coming up here from the outside, that the area was pretty much stuck in a time warp, and it was like 'Don't change anything,' " Barrett said, as he explained his initial impression of his new abode.[221]

Barrett attended Penn State University and has degrees in journalism and finance. His progressivism is a perspective rarely shared by the other callers on *WILK*. "I agree

---

221   Duke Barrett, interview by Kenny Luck, 25 April 2010.

that the station leans to the right because it seems that conservatives get their news from talk radio and *Fox News*, which I consider all commentary and propaganda," he said. "The vast majority of Middle America gets it from the other networks. And so, liberals tend to listen to a lot of different news sources, with the most informed getting it from National Public Radio and the least informed, at least by demographic studies, are those who listen to Fox News."[222]

Many *WILK* listeners and callers may take issue with the claim that the station is an outlet for much conservative anger in Northeastern Pennsylvania. Nevertheless, ample anecdotal evidence confirms this assertion. Whether conspiratorial, quoting from the Bible, or engaging in pseudo-intellectual banter, a rough approximation of *WILK* reveals that many callers are elderly, male, and conservative. "The demographics are white, elderly, over 60, American men," Barrett observed. "And that is a demographic that doesn't go well for advertising because there is no future in that."[223] The views expressed by many callers tend to represent a particular interest group, and not the populace as a whole, as you would be led to believe. News Commentator Sue Henry also recognized the demographic groups that compose *WILK*'s listenership. "A lot of the callers are men. A lot of them share a similar political philosophy. A lot of them are Republicans," she said. "Talk radio is the one medium that conservatives have managed to be successful at."[224]

Former *WILK* news commentator Kevin Lynn agrees with Barrett and Henry's observation. "The plurality of callers, more than any other percentage, are probably center-

222   Ibid.
223   Ibid.
224   Sue Henry, interview by Kenny Luck, 27 May 2010.

right," Lynn explained, after spending eight years as a host on the station. "I don't mean that about all callers. Some of them make really good points, but some of these people who call because they want to be heard and you could tell by their tone of voice from people that are not used to being listened to. I can also tell you if somebody calls if they're a preacher, because of the way that they talk."[225] The opinion that *WILK* listeners and callers are predominantly right-wing, older and male is not limited to just Barrett, Henry, and Lynn. Blogger Dan Spak also agrees. "There is absence on *WILK* of any views from the left. Anyone can agree with this," Spak argued. What is more, Spak points to *WILK*'s parent company as suspect. "Entercom Communications owns *WILK* and they seem to run right-wing formats. If you look at all the shows on *WILK* they are on the right or the radical right," he said.[226]

A casual look at *WILK* programming supports Spak's observation. Nearly all of the national shows represent a right-of-center viewpoint. This is evidenced by Rush Limbaugh and Michael Savage on the national level, and Sue Henry and most of her colleagues on a local level. When asked about the largely conservative programming, Henry hinted that it has more to do with company revenues than it does ideology. "It is a business model is what it is. It works in its form. Its success is due to the fact that it has advertising, and people are willing to buy advertising for talk radio," she said.[227]

Taking all of this into account, it is important to question the merits of *WILK*'s mission. If there is such a wide

---

225   Kevin Lynn, interview by Kenny Luck, 28 April 2010.
226   Dan Spak, interview by Kenny Luck, 12 April 2010.
227   Sue Henry, interview by Kenny Luck, 27 May 2010.

consensus that *WILK* caters to such a narrow demographic, why then do *WILK*, the callers, and hosts continue to claim that talk radio represents the views of the greater public, when clearly it does not? In many cases, the station is merely an outlet for opinion venting by cynical old men.

The Curious Case of Kevin Lynn

In April 2010, Kevin Lynn was fired after nearly a decade as a news commentator on *WILK*. "The interesting thing is the only person on the entire channel who was middle or to the left was Kevin Lynn," Spak said, as he described his reaction to Kevin Lynn's termination. "He actually held Republicans' feet to the fire, and challenged them when they would call in. He [talked] about Republican scandals, which was absent from every other show on the entire channel, and they got rid of him. How do you explain that?"[228] But when asked to comment about in an interview, Lynn was ambiguous and left the question unanswered. "There is nothing to walk through, and I am

> "I tried to joke with Webster if there was any corporate pressure coming over that he had to endorse this 'supplement for size' called Prolixus. It really shows what the demographics of these shows are."
>
> —*Duke Barrett*

228   Dan Spak, interview by Kenny Luck, 12 April 2010.

serious when I say that," he said, in a calm tone with an air of finality. "It is whatever it is, and I think that you should talk to them. I know what we discussed, and I know what I read in the newspaper the next day. I don't want you to get the wrong impression. I have plenty of things to say about Entercom, but I'm not going to say them to you." When it was revealed to Lynn the name of this subhead, he added: "For that you would have to have curious information, and I doubt they are going to give you any."[229]

Barrett, on the other hand, believes he knows what really happened behind Lynn's firing. "I think that there are people who, according to the rumor mill, used to continually call the management of that station and demand that Kevin Lynn be pulled," he explained. "Because of his progressive views, and because that people who couldn't get to the point or would make accusations not based on fact, he tended not to want to continue a conversation with them. He wanted to be serious. And so, I believe that a couple things happened. A decision had to be made. 'If we make a change with a gentleman like Webster who is a local institution, will he bring his audience along to *WILK*?' "[230]

They quick nature of Lynn's disappearance is illustrative. "The station brought him in and let him go," Barrett said, as he added more insight. "They made the decision to make the change. In such a public fishbowl, like how a lot of the media jobs are, these things are done very quickly. It is sort of like musical chairs where they take the needle off the record and everyone jumps. He did not go voluntarily. He was let go by the management."[231]

---

229   Kevin Lynn, interview by Kenny Luck, 28 April 2010.
230   Duke Barrett, interview by Kenny Luck, 25 April 2010.
231   Ibid.

WILK Program Director Nancy Kman could not be reached for comment. However, as reported by the *Citizen's Voice*, General Manager Ryan Flynn of Entercom Communications, who owns *WILK*, commented in the press: "This is a high-profile move that gives us the ability to expand the *WILK* brand and capitalize on the tremendous reputation of John Webster in this market."[232] As articulated by Barrett, "the station is trying to build a bigger audience, so to sell more ads, to get more revenue, and it becomes less of 'Let's have an even handed discussion,' as it is 'We just want to sell a lot more advertising to a lot of people,'" he said.[233] Flynn admitted to what Barrett had suggested: Webster's move to *WILK* was based more on the station's marketing interests, and not the quality of the shows.

A Biased Agenda

The inherent problem with news radio, as pointed out by Barrett and Spak, is that it blends news and commentary to where each entity becomes fused, and difficult to distinguish. The task of separating the host's interpretation from the objective factual evidence becomes almost impossible. Sue Henry's opinion of a news topic or event, for instance, is different from what the topic is actually about, but the two become inseparable in her mind, and probably in the minds of her devoted listeners. Of course, listeners are free to have whatever opinion they choose, but if one is willing to be at least minimally honest, why then is there such an over-representation of a conservative, male viewpoint on the *WILK*?

---

232   Stacy Brown, "Legal Issues Complicate Rock 107 Host's Switch to WILK," *The Citizen's Voice*, 1 April 2010.
233   Duke Barrett, interview by Kenny Luck, 25 April 2010.

Lynn recalled that during the run-up to the Iraq invasion during the spring of 2003, some of his criticisms about the war were suppressed by station managers. Although he noted, "Nobody ever came to me and said, 'You've got to talk this way,' " Lynn later made clear that his strong anti-war views were not welcomed at the station.[234] "Now with the Invasion of Iraq, which I was completely against from before the beginning and as it turns out, I was right for all the right reasons, there was a moment when everybody was waving flags and they were worried that I wasn't going to," he explained. "They did come to me and said, 'Well look, you just can't be against the war, or it's your ass because we are going in there. You are going to ruin things and we can't have you do that.' So I said, 'Okay, I'll be for the troops,' which was easy because I have no problem being for the troops."[235]

What is more, Barrett had a problem with former weekend host Barry Singer, whose show ran from roughly 2000–2006, for holding views contrary to Singer's. After Barrett argued that "the neo-cons had conned the public into the Iraq Invasion," Singer went the absurd lengths of calling Barrett at home to contest his claim. "Singer couldn't believe that I was putting forth such a theory, that he actually called all of the people with my last name in the Dallas area," Barrett recalled. "When I came home my wife said, 'Who is this Barry Singer guy? He called here looking for you and he thinks that you are part of some king of big political movement.' "[236]

Another controversy involved *WILK* host Sue Henry,

---

234   Kevin Lynn, interview by Kenny Luck, 28 April 2010.
235   Ibid.
236   Duke Barrett, interview by Kenny Luck, 25 April 2010.

although she denied that there was anything controversial about it. "There is not really much of a controversy there," she said.[237]

In an April 2006 *Citizen's Voice* editorial, writer Jim Spak (not to be confused with Dan Spak) accused Henry, who moonlights as *WRKC* general manger, of removing several shows from the King's College station because she "disagreed with their political opinions."[238] Shows such as *Radio Nation, Counter Spin,* and *Making Contact* all expressed a liberal perspective and Spak said that "after I complained to college officials about her actions, they saw no need to reverse her decision."[239] While quoting Spak's letter in an interview, Henry abruptly interjected. "You can stop right there!" she barked. "I don't want to go into this, but I will tell you that the FCC agreed with our position at *WRKC*. We are entitled to program our own radio decisions, and we are allowed to make decisions based upon what we believe."[240] By her own admission, Henry confirmed Spak's accusation inadvertently by failing to deny that her ideological leanings influenced her decision to cut these shows. "Spak was airing national shows," she continued. *"I did not agree with the agenda of these shows, and neither did the administration of King's College.* After that controversy, we used that space to launch a Hispanic language outreach show which, in the long run, is much more beneficial to the community in Northeastern Pennsylvania than any national show that is opinionated and divisive. We have got back to the mission of broadcasting which is serving the

237   Sue Henry, interview by Kenny Luck, 27 May 2010.
238   <http://gort42.blogspot.com/2006/04/radio-daze.html>
239   Ibid.
240   Sue Henry, interview by Kenny Luck, 27 May 2010.

The Layers of WILK FM

WILK FM NEWS RADIO

BIASED HOSTS

OLDER MALE CALLERS

RIGHT WING POLITICAL LEANINGS

community. His shows did not serve the community in any meaningful way."[241]

Fair enough. But how do national radio talk shows such as Rush Limbaugh and Michael Savage, which air daily on *WILK,* and are clearly "opinionated and divisive," serve the community? In accordance with Henry's rationale, if taken seriously and applied consistently, most of the programming at *WILK* would have to be replaced by other, less divisive shows. They fit her criteria of bad programming, so why doesn't she push for their eradication at her other employer, *WILK*? Rather than thinking of the issue this way, Henry attacked Spak. "It is one person trying to raise a stink because he was not happy with the programming decision. That is the way I see it. There is no controversy here. Move along."[242] She refused to comment further.

Henry is a fiscal conservative who bemoans government spending in all its guises—funds allocated to social services, unemployment, and the like. However, her stand is somewhat hypocritical, and ought to be called into question. During the 2008/2009 school year, for example, Henry and another colleague received an $181,000 grant from the government. The Kanjorski/Casey Congressionally-Elected Grant was awarded to Henry with the aim of expanding WRKC's signal. Although the money has benefited students at King's College, Henry—no matter what the purpose or outcome—has accepted money that, in the abstract, she opposes. By publically denouncing federal spending, yet taking government money for her own purposes, has she not violated her own principles?[243]

---

241   Ibid.
242   Ibid.
243   http://www.kings.edu/academicgrants/grantawards.htm

The Only Game in Town

Ultimately, the problem with *WILK* is not that it is a conservative radio station. The problem is that talk radio perpetuates controversies, and at times can even fabricate them by fueling a paranoid, largely male-dominated listenership. Many *WILK* callers mistakenly believe that their value system is representative of the rest of the way Northeastern Pennsylvania perceives reality. "It has the ability to raise people's awareness of what is important," said Henry.[244] Few would disagree with that. But what Henry and many of her like-minded callers consider "important" is quite debatable.

Meanwhile, Barrett hopes that Lynn's absence from *WILK* does not reduce the on-air dialogue to mere babble. "There is an entertainment factor and you have to get people to suddenly pay attention," Barrett said. "But you can do that in a practical way, or you could do it in a way that doesn't contribute to anything serious. I am hoping that the conversation is not dumbed-down so that it is chit-chat instead of debate," he added.[245] Finally, with its ability to disseminate opinions throughout Northeastern Pennsylvania, the quality and merit of these opinions is ultimately up to whoever decides to participate in the discussion. For now, to quote Barrett: *"WILK* is the only game in town."[246]

But in January 2010, a new station—WFTE FM—went on the air as a progressive alternative to WILK. WFTE's mission, as stated on its webpage, is to "create programming that serves the community and explores the information and ideas that are ignored, suppressed, overlooked or

244   Ibid.
245   Duke Barrett, interview by Kenny Luck, 25 April 2010.
246   Ibid.

underserved by the mainstream media in a region inundated with conservative talk shows, right-wing religious programs, and canned commercial music.[247] WILK—as well as other local radio personalities such as "Jumpin' Jeff Walker" and "Amanda" of WKRZ—fit the criteria of conservative talk and canned commercial music. WFTE is beginning to offer a different perspective to an underserved community and, perhaps, will begin to change of what the discourse in northeastern Pennsylvania looks and sounds like.

247   http://wfte.org/?p=82

eight

Political Corruption, Scandal, and the Breakdown of the Old NEPA Order

"It's the cash I'm worried about, Mike."
— **Robert Powell,** *Former Co-Owner of PA Child Care*

In recent years, myriad accusations, indictments, charges, and guilty pleas have been permeating the deepest layers of the Northeastern Pennsylvania political structure. This climate—one of male dominated nepotism—is controlled by the same families, with the same names, and continues to hold power as the rest of the population stands by quietly. Against this background of insider dealing, it is not hard to imagine how a corrupt culture can continue to flourish for generations without question or interruption.

In May 2010, the Interbranch Commission on Criminal Justice released its report on political corruption in

Luzerne County. The report explored the background of political corruption in Northeastern Pennsylvania. More specifically, it detailed what went wrong in the courtrooms of Michael Conahan and Mark Ciavarella—former judges who, in January 2009, had been accused of "sending thousands of juveniles to two private detention centers in exchange for $2.6 million in kickbacks."[248] Since then, the scandal has been headline news around the county and abroad, while gaining the attention of filmmaker Michael Moore, as well as other well-known media figures.[249]

With the ultimate fate of Ciavarella and Conahan still hanging in the balance, however, it is instructive to point out that the breakdown of the old NEPA order may finally fall with them. But the problem may be more than just two corrupt judges. Could it be that for the old order to fall, the antiquated ways of thinking must be abolished first?

The "Kids for Cash" Scandal

Perhaps the most nefarious of political crimes committed in Northeastern Pennsylvania, the "Kids for Cash" scandal, has proven Lord Acton's proverbial phrase to be true once again: "Power corrupts, but absolute power corrupts absolutely." News of the scandal prompted outrage from the public, and led many to ask questions: How could this happen? Are public officials trustworthy? What does this mean for the future of NEPA? The "Kids for Cash" scandal is context-sensitive. Therefore, it is important to remember that to answer the abovementioned questions,

---

248   Ian Urbina, "Despite Red Flags About Judges, A Kickback Scheme Flourished," *The New York Times*, 27 March 2009.
249   Dave Janoski, "Kids-for-cash Scandal Draws Attention of Filmmaker Moore," *The Times-Tribune*, 26 April 2010.

one must dissect the political culture of NEPA—what local media has referred to as a "culture of corruption"—and see what Ciavarella and Conahan's actions mean in a broader context.

Before federal prosecutors slapped the two judges with a 48-count indictment, which later dwindled, the judges, as reported by London's *The Guardian*, had a 26 percent sentencing rate for teenagers in 2004 at the height of the scandal.[250] Ciavarella claimed that he only sent children away who deserved it, but there was a clear connection between the beginning of the racket and a sharp increase in juvenile convictions.[251] Many of the children, who were aged between 10 and 17 years old, were sent away for frivolous reasons. For instance, one boy was put away for shooting out several windows with his BB gun even though the homeowner asked Ciavarella to go easy on him.[252] Another young girl was sentenced in January 2007 for creating a MySpace parody of her school vice-principal.[253] Ciavarella apparently did not find the prank amusing. "Adjudicated delinquent!" he yelled.

All of the sentenced minors were sent to a for-profit institution, PA Child Care, co-owned by Robert Powell. As reported by the *Citizen's Voice*, Powell admitted to paying the judges $770,000 for their help with sending children to the detention center where he stood to make a profit.[254] In

250   Ed Pilkington, "Jailed for a MySpace Parody, the Student Who Exposed America's Cash For Kids Scandal," *The Guardian*, 7 March 2009.
251   Ibid.
252   William Ecenbarger, "Luzerne's Youth-Court Scandal, "How? Why?" *The Philadelphia Inquirer*, 25 October 2009.
253   Ed Pilkington, "Jailed for a MySpace Parody, the Student Who Exposed America's Cash For Kids Scandal," *The Guardian*, 7 March 2009.
254   Dave Janoski and Michael Sisak, "This Time, for Keeps: Conahan Pleads Guilty to Single Count of Racketeering, Cannot Withdraw Plea If Unsatisfied with Sentence," *The Citizen's Voice*, 30 April 2010.

a recorded conversation, Powell said, "It's the cash I'm worried about, Mike."[255] Powell was clearly an important part of the alleged plan. In an ironic turn, Powell bought a yacht with his extra earnings and named it "Reel Justice." He spent many sunny afternoons on its deck, enjoying the warm weather while more than 70 children sat locked away in his private detention center.

After the initial news broke, the judges became entangled in a web of litigation. In February 2009, both Ciavarella and Conahan pleaded guilty. But six months later, the former judges withdrew their plea agreements, and after a Federal grand jury indicted them on 48 counts which included extortion and racketeering, Ciavarella and Conahan pleaded not guilty to the charges in a contrary move.[256] In March 2010, attorneys representing the judges attempted to move the trial out of state, arguing that the pre-trial publicity of the case was hurtful to their defendants' presumption of innocence. Before that was resolved, however, in a surprise move Conahan filed a new plea agreement in federal court.[257]

To date, the fate of the judges has not been determined. Yet the Machiavellian nature of their alleged crimes is worth noting. It is important to remember that Ciavarella and Conahan are part of a sociopolitical context that has been part of the NEPA landscape for decades. Getting rid of them is helpful, but an ideology that seems to resist change, that is very widespread, and that has become habitual in the minds of so many in Northeastern Pennsylvania must change.

---

255   Dave Janoski, "Game Plan," *The Citizen's Voice*, 12 May 2010.
256   Dave Janoski and Michael Sisak, "This Time, for Keeps: Conahan Pleads Guilty to Single Count of Racketeering, Cannot Withdraw Plea If Unsatisfied with Sentence," *The Citizen's Voice*, 30 April 2010.
257   Ibid.

Don Sherwood's Insatiable Libido

When former Congressman Don Sherwood won the U.S. House of Representatives seat in Pennsylvania's 10th District in late 1998, he was probably unaware that within one year he would meet someone who would change the course of his political career. Nine months after Sherwood was sworn into office, in September 1999, he met the lovely Cynthia Ore, a 23-year old Peruvian immigrant who apparently had an affinity for married politicians 35 years her senior.[258] A five year secret affair would take place that included all of the makings of a bad Hollywood drama: lawsuits involving millions of dollars, an extra-marital affair, scandal, and in the end, a disgraced public official. In 2006 Sherwood lost his congressional seat to Chris Carney, a former Defense Department Consultant and Navy Lieutenant Commander. He has since retreated back to Tunkhannock where the memory of his scandal has faded, as in the intervening years more attention has been given to the federal corruption probe.

Sherwood represents the caricature politician who, through his actions, captured the public imagination for a short while in 2005 and 2006. Sex scandals in Washington make for good gossip (e.g., former North Carolina Senator and vice-Presidential candidate John Edwards), but Sherwood was more than that. He seemed to embody contradictions: the politician who touted the "sanctity of marriage," but was involved in an on-going affair; the small town truck-driving American who became seduced by big city power enjoyed by elites. Finally, in an attempt to take

---

258   Dana Milbank, "Homo Politicus: The Strange and Scary Tribes that Run Our Government," 2008. www.danamilbank.com/sherwood.html (6 April 2010) as cited in.

back his image, Sherwood got caught in a semantic trap he set himself, claiming his innocence while simultaneously apologizing for actions he said he did not commit. As a politician, his religiosity—which by now no one could take seriously considering his actions while in office—and populist rhetoric won elections, but below the surface lay a more sinister reality.

As Sherwood's mistress, Ore once called the former congressman a "gentlemen" and said that he was "very charming."[259] She had met Sherwood at a Young Republicans meeting, and was smitten by the then 58-year congressman. The two soon became romantically and sexually involved, although Sherwood maintained that Ore was just a "casual acquaintance."[260] Ore, however, told a different story. As reported in a 2005 *Times Leader* article, she commented: "We went to movies, dinners. The wine and roses—that got me. I'm not someone to sleep around. With Don, it was exclusive."[261] It also did not help Sherwood's testimony

MEMORABLE MOMENTS

In 2002, two years before news of the sex scandal became public, Don Sherwood was named "Best Dressed Politician" by Politics PA.

259   Dana Milbank, "Homo Politicus: The Strange and Scary Tribes that Run Our Government."
<www.danamilbank.com/sherwood.html> (6 April 2010) as quoted in.
260   Ibid. As quoted in.
261   Kevin Amerman, "Sherwood a Charmer, Ore Recounts," *The Times Leader,* 8 August 2005.

when it was revealed that Ore had been co-habitating with the congressman at his Hill House apartment in Washington D.C.—an upper-class community where many congressmen live during the legislative season. "He always said you're my number one," Ore said. "He got on his knees many times just to kiss my hand. He called me his angel."[262]

Yet the good times could not last forever. As made clear by a document from the Superior Court of the District of Columbia's Civil Division, on the morning of June 24, 2004, "without any reason or justification,"[263] Sherwood began striking Ore "on her face, neck, chest and back with a closed fist."[264] The alleged attack would not be the last. "On or about September 22, 2004, Sherwood made repeated threats to physically harm Ore if she were to make any further attempt to inform the Metropolitan Police Department of the physical assaults Sherwood had committed on her," the document reported.[265] But the congressman denied these accusations. He argued that Ore's motives were political, and pointed out that she later backed off the claim. By contrast, Sherwood would later admit to the affair. "For about five years, I had an affair I deeply regret," he said, adding for good measure: "Although it was intermittent and ended last year, nothing I can say can diminish the pain and hurt I have caused my wife and family."[266]And although no one was charged in what police cited as a domestic incident, it was the beginning of Sherwood's public downfall.

---

262   Ibid.
263   Ore v. Sherwood, *Superior Court of the District of Columbia*, 15 June 2005.
264   Ibid.
265   Ibid.
266   Dana Milbank, "Homo Politicus: The Strange and Scary Tribes that Run Our Government," 2008
<www.danamilbank.com/sherwood.html> (6 April 2010) as quoted in.

Highlights of Corruption: All-Star Line-up

Mark Ciavarella

Also known as "Mr. Zero-tolerance," Ciavarella is a key figure in the "Kids-for-Cash' scandal who allegedly accepted more than 2.6 million dollars for sending children to a for-profit facility.

Michael Conahan

A former Luzerne County Judge, Conahan entered into a plea agreement in a federal court for his role in the "Kids-for-Cash" scandal.

Robert Mericle

The developer involved in the "Kids-for-Cash" scandal, Mericle allegedly paid a multi-million dollar "finder's fee" to Ciavarella and Conahan for their support of two juvenile detention centers he built.

Greg Skrepenak

A former NFL lineman and Luzerne County Commissioner, Skrepenak resigned in December 2009 after admitting to accepting a $5,000 bribe from a developer.

Richard Emanski

A carpet dealer who pleaded guilty in January 2010 for providing a Wilkes-Barre Area School Board member with a free rug in exchange for his help securing a school district contract.

Robert Cordaro

A former Lackawanna County commissioner who was charged by federal prosecutors in March 2010 for his involvement in dubious contract dealings that generated at least $475,000 in kickbacks.

A.J. Munchak

The current Lackawanna County minority commissioner who, like Cordaro, is charged with allegedly receiving kickbacks for his involvement in unethical contract dealings.

Throughout 2005 and 2006, the story drifted in and out of the media. By the time the 2006 mid-term elections approached, Sherwood was ready to seek forgiveness. He went into the 2006 election with the support of President Bush, and played down the Ore incident. When Chris Carney, Sherwood's opponent, ran a television ad reminding voters of the affair, Sherwood responded. "While I am truly sorry for disappointing you, I never wavered from my commitment to reduce taxes, create jobs and bring home our fair share," he said.[267] Sherwood lost the election.

The story did not end there, however. Shortly before the election, it was revealed that Sherwood refused to pay Ore "$500,000 in a settlement reached in November 2005 that contained a powerful incentive for her to keep quiet until after Election Day."[268] In other words, it appeared that Sherwood was paying Ore hush money to keep her quiet until November 7, 2006—Election Day. As if having an affair, denying it, and later coming clean weren't enough, Sherwood now claimed that Ore violated a confidentially clause in their agreement, and was not entitled to the rest of the money. After the election, the disgraced congressman quietly faded into the background, returning to his car dealership in Tunkhannock. And although years later his scandal has been nearly forgotten, it is important to remember Sherwood's hypocrisy and scandal.

Pay-to-Play Politics and the Federal Probe

After spending six years in the National Football League (NFL), Greg Skrepenak—a University of Michigan gradu-

267   <http://www.youtube.com/watch?v=8D303Zo3nlk>
268   Michael Rubinkam, "Republican Congressman Paid Mistress Hush Money" *The Associated Press*, 4 November 2006.

ate and Gator Bowl co-MVP—came back home to North-eastern Pennsylvania to bask in an all-American fanfare. In 2003, Skrepenak was elected Democratic Commissioner of Luzerne County, and easily won re-election in 2007. But by the time he resigned in December 2009, he was just one more fallen, corrupt public official in Northeastern Pennsylvania.[269]

Skrepenak's problems were not limited to an unhealthy diet and a bulging waistline. The monstrous former line-backer was charged with "accepting a $5,000 bribe from a developer for voting to accept a developer's project into a government funded tax incentive program."[270] Initially, Skrepenak claimed that he did not realize he did anything unethical until he met with the authorities. It was then when he admitted that he was "truly sorry for this turn of events."[271] In another strange turn, Skrepenak was also, as reported by the *Standard Speaker,* "one of two commission-ers who signed a controversial $58 million, 20-year lease with a for-profit detention center at the heart of the 'Kids for Cash' scandal."[272] Skrepenak would not be the first or the last to be charged in Luzerne County. He is now serving a two year sentence for his crimes. As of January 2010, *The Associated Press* reported that 23 people in Luzerne County have been charged in what they call "unrelated schemes."[273] This includes Ciavarella, Conahan and Skrepenak, but oth-

---

269   Michael R. Sisak, "Skrepenak to Resign amid 'Mistakes,'" *The Standard Speaker,* 17 December 2009.

270   Michael R. Sisak and Dave Janoski, "Luzerne Commissioner Skrepenak Resigns and will Plead Gulity," *News Bank: America's Newspapers,* 18 December 2009.

271   Michael R. Sisak, "Skrepenak to Resign amid 'Mistakes,'" *The Standard Speaker,* 17 December 2009.

272   Ibid.

273   <http://www.msnbc.msn.com/id/35046453/ns/us_news-crime_and_courts/>

ers such as a school superintendent, school board members, and other courthouse officials have also been charged.[274] The corruption is widespread, and endemic. Even Lackawanna County became infected with crimes and unethical behavior by high political officials.

Four months after Skrepenak's crimes were exposed, two commissioners in neighboring Lackawanna County—Robert Cordaro and A.J. Munchak—were indicted for engaging in dubious contract negotiations which allegedly yielded thousands of dollars in kickbacks.[275] Cordaro, who was also a football player like Skrepenak (Cordaro was a linebacker at Dunmore High School in the late 1970s), was voted out of office in 2008, although Munchak stayed on as Republican minority commissioner through the time the indictments were issued. Months later, both Munchak and Cordaro pleaded not guilty in a Federal Court in Wilkes-Barre.[276]

The 40 count indictment facing Munchak and Cordaro is, to use one commissioner's words, "frankly staggering."[277] If convicted they both face between 193 to 364 years in prison. They are just the most recent public officials to be charge in a string of corruption in the past two years. It remains to be seen how many more politicians will be exposed.

A Mis-*education*

The corruption and unethical conduct within Luzerne County is not limited to a few judges or politicians; the

---

274   Ibid.
275   Joe McDonald, "Cordero, Munchak Indicted," *The Citizen's Voice*, 17 March 2010.
276   Joe McDonald, "Cordaro, Munchak Arraigned," The Citizen's Voice, 19 March 2010.
277   Ibid.

school districts have also become infected. Moreover, it appears that public officials in any capacity—whether governmental, educational, or judicial—are all part of the same sickening, broken system within Luzerne County. According to the *Philadelphia Inquirer*, as of November 2009, six school board members in Luzerne County had been indicted on charges that they accepted bribes in exchange for hiring teachers in their district.[278] For instance, the most emblematic among corrupt school officials in the region is former Wilkes-Barre Area School Board President Frank Pizzalla Jr., who has served as school board president since 2007.

Pizzalla, who was indicted in September 2009, allegedly passed "a bribe to a sitting board member from the relative of a person seeking a teaching job in 2004."[279] But in a move of incredible audacity, while maintaining his innocence, Pizzalla was re-elected president of the Wilkes-Barre School Board in December 2009 by a vote of 6 to 1.[280] The appropriate action would have been to step down, however, Pizzalla did not. The mere appearance of impropriety in a climate of corruption is enough of a reason to voluntarily step down. Two Wilkes-Barre Area board members—Mary Ann Toole and Robert M. Corcoran—abstained from the vote. "I couldn't in good conscience vote for him because of the indictment," Toole said, commenting on Pizzalla's rather unfortunate re-election to the school board.[281] In

---

278   William Ecenbarger, "In Pa. Coal Region, a Mother Lode of Corruption," *The Philadelphia Inquirer*, 16 November 2009.
279   Mark Guydish, "Dunn Says He's Guilty of Bribe," *The Times Leader*, 17 December 2009.
280   Janine Ungvarsky, "Indicted Pizzella Heads to W-B Area," *The Times Leader*, 8 December 2009.
281   Ibid.

February 2010, Pizzalla signed a plea agreement with federal prosecutors, but "did not identify the specific charge to which he pleaded guilty."[282] He would not be the only school-related employee charged in Wilkes-Barre.

Jeffrey Piazza, a former Wilkes-Barre Area Career and Technical Center employee, like Pizzalla, entered a plea in federal court. Piazza's crime, however, was different. He was charged with a felony count of mail fraud. According to a report by the *Times Leader*, Piazza "conspired with a vendor who supplied technology equipment to the center to inflate the prices of the equipment so that kickbacks could be paid [to him]."[283] The vendor was Intellacom Inc. In April 2010, Piazza was sentenced to six months in prison after admitting to "taking at least $16,600 in kickbacks."[284] A newspaper reported that during his sentencing in front of Judge James Munley at the Federal Courthouse in Scranton, Piazza never "directly apologized for his crime."[285]

And then there is Brian Dunn. In a nauseating admittance of guilt, Dunn "pleaded guilty to accepting a $5,000 bribe from the relative of a person who got a teaching job in the school district."[286] Dunn was a former school board member at Wilkes-Barre Area, and has no education "beyond a high school diploma."[287] In a self-serving rhetorical move, Dunn made a phony "apology" while in court. "I made a mistake and I am deeply sorry for the embarrassment I

---

282   Terrie Morgan-Besecker, "W-B Area Head Signs Plea Deal," *The Times-Leader*, 3 February 2010.
283   Sheena Delazio, "Ex-school Worker's Time in Fraud Case Likely 4 – 10 months," *The Times-Leader*, 30 December 2009.
284   Terrie Morgan-Besecker, "Piazza's Mail Fraud: 6 Months," *The Times-Leader*, 1 April 2010.
285   Ibid.
286   Mark Guydish, "Dunn Says He's Guilty of Bribe," *The Times-Leader*, 17 December 2009.
287   Ibid.

caused my family and my friends," Dunn said, while standing in front of U.S. District Judge Richard Conaboy.[288]

Apologizing for the embarrassment he caused his family and friends may be nice, but what about the pain and trouble he caused to others, such as honest job seekers and the public? Should he apologize to the latter groups first, rather than focus on his immediate cohorts? Dunn is one of three Wilkes-Barre Area board members facing federal corruption charges, which includes Pizzalla and another former Wilkes-Barre Area School Board President, James Height.

According to the Philadelphia Inquirer, "based on indictments and subsequent guilty pleas, the going rate for a teaching job is $5,000 in the Wilkes-Barre Area School District and the Hanover Area School District."

---

288   Ibid.

The Oliveri Ordeal

In December 2009, the same month Pizzalla was voted back for another term as president of the Wilkes-Barre school board, former Pittston Area School Board President Joseph Oliveri was charged for "accepting money in exchange for helping a contractor get work in the district."[289] According to newspaper reports, he was the second school official from Pittston Area to be charged by federal prosecutors.[290] Former superintendent Ross Scarantino had pleaded guilty in October 2009 "for accepting money in exchange for helping a contractor obtain business within the district."[291]

Interestingly, Oliveri's son had worked at Intellacom, Inc.—the same company tied to Jeffery Piazza's mail fraud scheme. In April 2007, Oliveri awarded Intellacom with a $269,192 no-bid contract.[292] What is more, "Federal prosecutors have previously taken records related to Intellacom from several other school districts, including the Wilkes-Barre Area Technical Center, Pittston Area, Wyoming Valley West, and Luzerne County Community College."[293]

Craig Sterling—an employee at Intellacom—was fired in January 2010 after it was revealed that he was involved in Piazza's crimes. The U.S. Attorney's Office charged Sterling with one count of mail fraud.[294] Sterling's attorney, Elizabeth Lippy, admitted: "[Sterling] is a small piece of a

---

289   Edward Lewis, "Ex-Pittston Area Board President to Face Sentencing," *The Times-Leader*, 8 December 2010.
290   Ibid.
291   Terrie Morgan-Beseker, "Ex-PA Director Oliveri Sentenced," *The Times-Leader*, 2 February 2010.
292   Ibid.
293   Terrie Morgan-Besecker, "Intellacom Linked to Mail Fraud Charge," *The Times-Leader*, 30 March 2010.
294   Ibid.

big puzzle."[295] The puzzle included Oliveri, and the afore-mentioned district administrators.

Meanwhile, when it was time for Oliveri to face U.S. District Judge Thomas I. Vanaskie for sentencing, he commented: "I honestly didn't think I did anything wrong."[296] Vanaskie was not persuaded. He slapped Oliveri with a 12 month and one day prison sentence along with a $3,000 fine. The *Times Leader* reported that Assistant U.S. Attorney William Houser noted that "Oliveri's actions were indicative of the 'culture of corruption' that has permeated Luzerne County's government."[297]

School's Out

"The harsh truth," said Thomas Baldino, a Wilkes University college professor, "is that it costs a least a couple thousand dollars to get a job in a school district around here. You either pay it or you go well outside the area."[298] With more than 72 local governments in Luzerne County—including boroughs, cities, and townships—a legacy of the coal era, corruption thrives unimpeded.[299] The problem is, of course, with such an array of governing units, the potential for corruption also increases. Local governments and school districts get caught in a game of "who-knows-who," while students, educators, and the public are the ones who ultimately lose.

---

295   Ibid.
296   Terrie Morgan-Beseker, "Ex-PA Director Oliveri Sentenced," *The Times-Leader*, 2 February 2010.
297   Ibid.
298   William Ecenbarger, "In Pa. Coal Region, a Mother Lode of Corruption," *The Philadelphia Inquirer*, 16 November 2009.
299   Ibid.

Pennsylvania's "crook-of-the-month club," coined after former Governor Milton J. Shapp's administration had more than 60 convictions in the 1960s, continues to evolve, producing generations of frauds, crooks, and hucksters.[300] With each charge and indictment, the public's confidence in their governing system dwindles; it remains to be seen how many more public officials will fall to greed and corruption, but a good guess is that the worst has yet to be revealed.

---

300   Joe Pilchesky, "A Not-So-Proud History" *The Patriot News*, 15 November 2009.

Frank Pizzalla Jr.

Former Wilkes-Barre Area School Board President charged with passing a bribe to a school board member in 2004.

Jeffery Piazza

Former Wilkes-Barre Area Career and Technical Center employee charged with mail fraud.

Brian Dunn

Former Wilkes-Barre Area school board member who accepted a $5,000 bribe from a teacher's relative for a job.

James Height

Former Wilkes-Barre Area school board president who accepted $2,000 from a contractor seeking district business.

Allen Bellas

Former Wyoming Valley West school board member who accepted a bribe for getting a contractor approved for a tax-forgiveness program.

nine

Gas & Greed

"The destruction to the very foundations of our American system—our democracy—is one of the things that concern me the most. Our basic individual rights that we hold as Americans are being compromised... the act of a huge corporation [being] able to dismantle our most basic public and environmental laws [is] destructive to the core of our democracy."

—Josh Fox, *Filmmaker*

Activist Sarah Gaia (who requested that her real name not be used) recalled when, in 2006, the first "land men" began to appear in Northern Tier of Pennsylvania. The men were charming, well groomed and assured all that they wouldn't be around for long. "When they first came, they said: 'There might be some gas here. We are just looking. So we will drill a well and you will never know that we were here,'" the young activist recalled.[301] They made what they were doing seem so innocent, so simple. But one year later the first well was drilled, the land men, it seemed,

---

301   Sarah Gaia, interview by Kenny Luck, 10 May 2010.

could not get enough. After several wells were already
drilled, one land man allegedly said: "All we are going to
do is drill another well, get the gas, and then we will plant
a Christmas tree." Gaia pointed out the reality of the situation. "They said that they were going to drill a well every 670
acres. Right now there are 63 wells in nine square miles."[302]

Two prominent companies operating in the region—
Cabot Oil and Gas and Chesapeake Energy—have been at
the center of the recent debate. Asked to go on the record,
George Stark, the Director of External Affairs for Cabot,
commented: "Let me get a piece of paper so that I will be
ready."[303] Stark's responses were read verbatim from a company issued piece of paper. This was for a simple media inquiry. When asked how many wells were drilled, Stark's stiff
answers turned even more hesitant. "I believe at this point...
I can't do the math off the top of my head. We are probably...
I don't know. What I can tell you is in 2008, 20 wells were
drilled and last year we had nearly 40 wells drilled," he ut-
tered. "I am not sure what we have planned in 2010."[304] The
truth is there was more drilling planned for 2010—and beyond. When the same general media inquiry was requested
from Chesapeake, Rory Sweeney, Media Relations Coordi-
nator, refused to go on the record. Rather, he insisted on
sending an email with a list of company-approved talking
points. In a revealing moment, as the conversation continued, Sweeney's already skeptical tone of voice turned
somewhat aggressive, when asked general questions about
the company's operations in Susquehanna County. Overall,
he was evasive and noncommittal in the few answers that

---

302   Ibid.
303   George Stark, interview by Kenny Luck, 11 May 2010.
304   Ibid.

were given. A few days later, in the email he sent, Sweeney admitted: "Regarding your inquiry regarding our plans in Susquehanna County, we have a significant leasehold there and plan to develop it."[305]

As both companies continue to drill more wells, the damaging environmental effects caused by the drilling remain clear. In April 2010, Pennsylvania's Department of Environmental Protection banned Cabot from drilling new wells in Dimock Township.[306] Speaking for the company, Stark refused to link Cabot directly to the spill. "There is an area surrounding Dimock Township where we are halting our efforts to drill in a nine square mile area. We are working to investigate the presence of methane in the aquifer," he said, while not admitting that there already was methane in the water supply.[307]

According to Gaia, Cabot insisted to their investors that the ban "will have insignificant to zero effect on our operating."[308] What is more, Cabot has already been sued over other accidents in the area. "In Dimock, there was a lawsuit. The plaintiffs did win where Cabot has to install water buffalos to each house because they can't drink their water or bathe in it," said Gaia. "But in the winter, those water buffalos freeze, so Cabot does not have to pay for the heating bills. Some people's gas bills doubled or quadrupled and they couldn't afford to pay it. So they have no water."[309]

The drilling industry maintains that natural gas burns

305   Rory Sweeney, "Media Inquiry," 14 May 2010, personal e-mail (14 May 2010).
306   http://citizensvoice.com/news/cabot-ban-inspires-county-partnership-1.732108
307   http://www.propublica.org/feature/frack-fluid-spill-in-dimock-contaminates-stream-killing-fish-921
308   Sarah Gaia, interview by Kenny Luck, 10 May 2010.
309   Ibid.

cleaner, so it is an improvement over coal and other fossil fuels. And although that claim is true, the process of extracting natural gas is a much dirtier process, and it is unclear if the benefits outweigh the costs. With parts of the Delaware River Basin turned into a virtual gas field, and with several gas spills that contaminated some of the water supply already, it is important that all of the facts be made available before the public should decide if the drilling ought to continue.

Gas Land

After Filmmaker Josh Fox received a lease in the mail at his Milanville, Pennsylvania, home he decided to do some investigation into the nature of the gas drilling that had been taking place in the northern counties. "I found out about the major exceptions to all of the major environmental laws that the drilling companies have," Fox said. "I immediately got suspicious. I went to Dimock first because it's close. I found that place turned upside down and destroyed. The water was unusable [and], their animals and children were getting sick. It was turned into an industrial zone. To

"We have not seen the extent of drilling in the last 30 years to what you are seeing in the past three years. Our goal is to get that gas out and to put it into market.

—*George Stark,*
Director of External Affairs,
Cabot Oil and Gas

think of that kind of activity happening in the Delaware River Basin was very shocking to me."[310]

There is little regulation to monitor the practices of the oil and gas industry in Pennsylvania to date. For example, according to a *New York Times*, a 2005 energy bill, which former Vice-President Dick Chaney endorsed, "stripped the Environmental Protection Agency of its authority to regulate a drilling process called 'hydraulic fracturing.'"[311] What is more, in October 2010, Harrisburg politicians failed to pass a Marcellus Shale Severance Tax that would have placed at least some responsibility on companies such as Cabot and Chesapeake. Rather than getting regulations, environmentalists, homeowners, and concerned citizens got nothing and will, according to former Governor Ed Rendell, have to "wait another year."[312]

Hydraulic fracturing, the controversial practice used in extracting natural gas, takes a mixture of sand, water, and chemicals and forces them at very high pressure down into a well. The compound then breaks up the shale below, and releases the gas. But there are problems. "Eighty percent of the fracturing fluid stays underground and never resurfaces," Gaia said, as she explained her concerns over the extracting process. "So we don't know where it goes. But the 15 to 20 percent that does come back up are placed in what's called collection ponds, but they're really toxic waste pits. It's basically a hole dug in the ground that is lined with hefty bags. All of the chemicals that they use are known to be dermatological and neurological toxins. Children can fall into it, animals

310   Josh Fox, interview by Kenny Luck, 12 May 2010.
311   http://www.nytimes.com/2009/11/03/opinion/03tue3.html
312   Robert Swift, "Severance Tax Dies," *The Citizen's Voice*, 22 October 2010.

Perspectives on Natural Gas Drilling

"They had a diesel spill. Eight thousand gallons of diesel spilled into the water. The Dimmock Creek dumps into the Tunkhannock Creek, which comes down into the Lackawanna River which comes down into Lake Scranton. That is where most of Scranton gets their drinking water. Think about that for awhile."

—*Sarah Gaia*, Activist

"I think the process has to be very, very heavily regulated—if not banned in extremely sensitive watershed areas. I think there is huge problems with the air admission; huge problems with water contamination; huge problems with the land—all of that has to stop. We are in a situation where there is so much evidence on the ground. There are so many people saying, 'this is what is happening to me!'"

—*Josh Fox*, Director "Gas Land"

"We have an ordinance here in Dish, TX, but our council is so small that it really doesn't help all that much. So, the drilling companies go just outside of our borders. There is a home just inside of our border. These folks started getting some sediment in their water. It got to the point where they thought it was bad enough to get a filtration system for the house. So the last six or eight months have been fine. But last Tuesday, the lady called me and it had got so bad it has completely clogged up their water system. They can't get any pressure for their water. It has essentially made their water system useless."

—*Calvin Tillman*, Mayor, Dish, Texas

"My friend is a teacher at Elk Lake School District, and she said it is terrible and destructive—these loud trucks, these loud drills and the bright lights—and every once in awhile you see this fire burning off these big pipes. It's scary sometimes. It has really changed in a year over there."

—***Kim Marco***, Resident and Landowner

have. They don't have to fence them off or anything."[313]

After seeing the effects of hydraulic fracturing and other methods used by the oil and gas industry in Susquehanna County, Fox decided to make a documentary film which explores the consequences of natural gas drilling. One year later, *Gas Land* began screenings across the region and county. According to Fox, audiences have been very receptive. "It has been unbelievable," he explained. "Everywhere the film goes it has been sold out and getting standing ovations. The reception is overwhelming. Last night in Williamsport, PA, we had 1,200 people show up to see the film. That is three percent of the population of Williamsport!"[314]

The film has been shown on both PBS and HBO, and for his efforts, Fox was awarded the Special Jury Prize for Documentary at the Sundance Film Festival Awards. When asked how the oil and gas companies responded to the film, Fox said: "I don't think they took it very seriously. But I also think that their policy is not to talk with anybody. I am not sure if it was that they did not want to be on camera, or if they did not take the film itself seriously because it's independent."[315]

Others in the oil and gas industry have taken offense to the film. Fox said that The Independent Wyoming Gas Association of New York has attacked him. "They are fond of saying: 'Watching this film is like watching airplane crash footage and determining that the airline industry is unsafe.' But if the industry, by its own admission, has a two to five percent well failure rate—if two to five percent planes crashed—we would have no airplanes. No one would ever

---

313   Sarah Gaia, interview by Kenny Luck, 10 May 2010.
314   Josh Fox, interview by Kenny Luck, 12 May 2010.
315   Ibid.

get on a plane. Their arguments are specious, and at worse they are outright lies. So they haven't been challenging me openly in the public."[316]

Still, the film seems to be having an impact. "I think it is raising awareness," Fox said, while reflecting up the impact of his work. "The oil and gas industry doesn't have to tell you that your water can be contaminated. They don't have to tell you the air will be polluted and your health can be compromised. They don't have to tell you that your land will be destroyed. My film is telling the story of what is actually happening out there, so that people can make informed decisions. But also, it is about exposing an injustice that is happening out there in America that shouldn't be happening, that hopefully we could correct."[317]

Undercut Tactics

As the mayor of Dish, Texas, Calvin Tillman has been immersed in a constant war with the oil and gas companies, and he is trying to prevent the same thing from happening in Pennsylvania. "As a small town mayor I've had to deal with that for a number of years," Tillman said, as he spoke from his Texas home. "I've been successful in getting some relief for my citizens. Our battle here has become really public. The thing I tell people here is, 'don't let it happen to you. Don't let what happened here happen there.' "[318]

Tillman is a nagging gadfly—at least from the perspective of the oil and gas companies—and has had to fight tirelessly for the interests of his citizens against the looming corporate monoliths. The oil and gas companies have even

---

316　Ibid.
317　Ibid.
318　Calvin Tillman, interview by Kenny Luck, 11 May 2010.

devoted space for him in their weekly *Barnett Shale News-letter*. Although Texas is more than one thousand miles away, the citizens of Dish and Susquehanna County have a lot in common: They are both targets of unethical practices. "Unfortunately, there is a lot of social injustice that goes on," Tillman explained. "They seized the opportunity in the most rural, most economically depressed areas—the areas where folks need money. Some of these folks are on the verge of losing their homes and they think it's God sent when the guy shows up with a checkbook. At the end of the day, they end up losing their water or air quality and certainly their way of life has changed dramatically from what it once was."[319]

Gaia agrees, and began seeing a similar pattern developing in places like Dimock, PA. She believes that many

> "Like any industry, there are good players and there are bad players. There are always ethical players, and there are those who are not ethical and try to cut corners. It's the same with the gas industry. Our laws and regulations in the United States support resource extraction. So these guys think that the law is on their side. But for five or ten years, it is going to be a real mess up there. All we can do is work towards making sure our legislatures pass the proper regulations now to protect us if an environmental problem happens."
>
> —*Paul Lumia, North Branch Land Trust*

---

319   Ibid.

people who have leased their land for drilling have been somewhat misled. "There are a lot of people now that regret signing," Gaia said. "Others are like, 'You've signed it. It's your fault.' If these people knew what was coming, they would not have signed it. They were so manipulated. The companies preyed on people in this area, on poverty, on people who were not educated about it. Most of the people are farmers. They are good people, and they are good at what they do, but they don't know geology. They don't know legalese. They don't know any of these things, so they were very easily preyed upon. It's terrible."[320]

One person who reluctantly signed a lease was Kim Marco. A landowner who lives just outside of Thompson, PA, Marco said that her and her husband felt "bullied" into signing their mineral rights over to a private corporation. "We are landlocked by these two brothers who own the land around us," she said. After her neighbors signed off, Marco and her husband felt that their options were limited. "The company contacted us and said, 'You know, we do have the rights within so many feet to suck it from underneath your land anyway.' That's how we felt bullied. They were going to take it if our neighbors signed and found the gas."[321]

Throughout the discussion, Marco continuously expressed concern for the negative effects that may emerge as a result of the drilling. "My friend brought this point up. She said: 'I have daughters and there is going to be all kind of guys living in trailers around my land. I don't want strangers on my property.' "[322] As a mother of five, Marco

---

320   Sarah Gaia, interview by Kenny Luck, 10 May 2010.
321   Kim Marco, interview by Kenny Luck, 16 May 2010.
322   Ibid.

said that it could be a little unnerving having strangers around her property at all hours. In an earlier discussion, Gaia explained the work cycle of many of the workers. "Most of the people who work here are from the Midwest. They're here, and come for a week or so. I believe they work 14 days on and 14 days off, if I'm not mistaken. On their days off they fly back home to Texas; they fly back to Oklahoma. They're not that worried about what our water is like. They don't care. Their families don't live here, their children don't have to drink the water. If you were living in it, you would think differently."[323]

Another problem Marco recognizes, which has been noted by Gaia and Tillman, is the demographics of Susquehanna County. "I think we are the second or third poorest county, and it is exciting to people because it's a struggling county," Marco said.[324] As of late, however, she has been hearing negative accounts of people in her town that are having trouble with companies like Cabot Oil and Gas and Chesapeake Energy. "There are farmers in the Elk Lake region that did try to sue these companies because they felt like they came in under false pretenses. The companies were offering them [one] rate, and making it sound like it was so great and then the next year people are getting double and triple what they were offered. But after you sign a contract there isn't much you can do."[325]

Like Marco, Gaia has heard disturbing stories emerging out of Susquehanna County involving questionable business practices. "They told people that if they don't sign

---

323   Sarah Gaia, interview by Kenny Luck, 10 May 2010.
324   Kim Marco, interview by Kenny Luck, 16 May 2010.
325   Ibid.

then they wouldn't come back," Gaia explained.[326] "But that was completely untrue. They're awful. They are sneaky and tricky. They have different subsidiary companies, so they are very good with sneaking around. These are some of the things that they have been saying. 'You don't need a lawyer, just sign the lease. You don't need to worry about that. It's standard. All of your neighbors have signed so if you don't, they are just going to take your gas anyway and then you are not going to get any money for it.' "[327] The point is that time and again, residents and landowners of Susquehanna County seem to be getting ripped off by corporations who operate using shadowy practices.

An Industrial Juggernaut

"There's no way from trying to stop that juggernaut from staying in the Northern Tier of Pennsylvania," said Paul Lumia, Executive Director of North Branch Land Trust (NBLT). "There are a lot of people that want us to stop the drilling and that train has left the station years ago. And so, we advocate for super strict regulations that protect the land owners, and communities. If you want to come to our town and take our gas then you do it the right way, and leave it the way you found it once you pull out. That's what we advocate for."[328]

The NBLT is a non-profit organization that has been operating in more than eight counties since 1993, and has helped preserve 10,000 acres of land across Pennsylvania. Through Conservation Edens, land owners can set aside their land to protect it from development. As Lumia points

326   Sarah Gaia, interview by Kenny Luck, 10 May 2010.
327   Ibid.
328   Paul Lumia, interview by Kenny Luck, 17 May 2010.

out, gas companies continue to find ways to work around these protections. "If there is a Conservation Eden on a property, the gas companies can't lease land to put a gas well to put on the property," he said. "But they can lease the land with a no development lease, meaning they can put a drill rig on an adjacent property and drill underneath horizontally onto the land that has a Conservation Eden."[329]

Lumia believes that the oil and gas industries will be in operating in Pennsylvania for a long time. "The bottom line is that it is a game changer for the region," he said, while discussing the impact of the drilling. "People weren't expecting the amount of industrial operations that is starting to happen. It is going to get a lot bigger. You are going from a very rural and agrarian region to a super industrial operation taking place. So, people are a little shocked at what they see even though they signed onto it."[330]

As experience shows, the problem for many people living in the Northern Tier will be how they adjust to the transformation that has already begun to take place in the region. As more time passes, and small towns like Susquehanna began to have their economy transformed by the oil and gas industry, it seems clear that there is no turning back. According to Lumia, one indication which will reveal how long the companies plan on staying is the amount of money they invest. "Chesapeake spent like 40 million dollars signing up new land owners," he said. "That is serious money. It shows you that this is real, and they are not just going to walk away from it. They've got too much invested already."[331] If this is the case, one question presents itself:

329   Ibid.
330   Ibid.
331   Ibid.

What can be done to force companies like Cabot Oil and Gas and Chesapeake Energy to engage in better business practices, reinvest in the communities they are changing, and take more responsibility to protect the environment?

Pennsylvania's landscape has already been scarred by industry in the past. In the late nineteenth and early twentieth centuries, the coal barons destroyed the environment and many people's quality of life as they tried to quench their insatiable thirst for more wealth, and more resources. In the end, it has taken nearly 100 years to clean up their mess, and the scars that the surrounding land still wears are testament to this sad legacy of greed and irresponsibility. Can we afford to stand by as yet another generation of coal barons enters into the region to rape the land? How the public perceives this problem and legislatures deal with it will inevitably define Pennsylvania's Northern Tier for generations to come.

In the meantime, people like Gaia continue to fight for more regulations to protect people and the land. "We really need to have a total paradigm shift just in our thinking. Is the extraction of this resource worth all of the other things that are going to happen?" But fighting a multi-billion dollar industry is no easy task. "Anybody that is going to make money on the situation is going to promote it," she said, "and they are going to ignore the bad things. And people that don't have to live with that they are doing are going to obviously dismiss the side effects."[332]

---

332   Sarah Gaia, interview by Kenny Luck, 10 May 2010.

Conclusion:

Are You NEPATIZED?

"This is not the time to suspend our critical thinking faculties. Rather, it is the time to apply these faculties to the immediate people and events around us—which is the primary aim of this book. The people of Northeastern Pennsylvania have a critical choice about the future: Do we allow our social and political institutions to be run by fraudulent hucksters, fanatical demagogues, and faux experts, or do we seek a new understanding by applying different ways of thinking to the current state of affairs?"

—Kenny Luck, *Author*

As I worked on this book, I would sometimes get distracted, but continued to ask: "Who cares?" and "What's your point?" to get myself back in line. These two questions are a writer's best tool to have in his or her arsenal. Asking self-criticizing questions avoids needless digressions and diatribes. In most cases, these questions answered themselves: I am writing a book about the people, events, and controversies in my home region, and attempting to interpret the meaning of these things in a larger, "big picture" context.

"NEPATIZED" is a neologism—newly created word— that describes and defines the diverse, unique, and, at times, outrageous features of Northeastern Pennsylvania. These features, however, are nothing to celebrate, as shown throughout this book. As a verb, NEPATIZE can describe the actions of a person. But it can also act as a modifier, describing a person or action as in: "His thinking has become *NEPATIZED*." I like to believe that the word describes the state of mind, the *zeitgeist* if you will, of a collectivity of people.

A more formal definition might look like this:

NEPATIZE |ˈnēpəˌtīz|
[as adjective] **nepatized**
1.   referring to the actions of public officials while engaging in unlawful, unethical, or immoral conduct.
2.   referring to a system of outdated beliefs held by residents of Northeastern Pennsylvania.
3.   referring to the anti-intellectual babble often heard on local talk radio programs.
4.   referring to a NEPA-centric worldview, wherein one believes that Northeastern Pennsylvania is literally at the center of the world.

Some in the media have referred to Northeastern Pennsylvania as "NEPOTIZED" or "NEPOTISTIC." I reject these terms because they are narrowly constructed, and only apply to a select group of corrupt public officials. Nepotism is certainly a widespread problem in region, but I am more interested in subjects outside of corruption and family ties. I am interested in the underlying *thinking* behind these nefarious actions. Probing the psychology of the region is certainly outside the scope of this book, but my aim is to illuminate Northeastern Pennsylvania's core beliefs through case studies of corruption, fraud, bigotry, and outright idiocy.

~

A land settled by immigrants, Northeastern Pennsylvania has maintained an outmoded mentality—brought by the Polish, Irish, Germans, Italians, and others—that has outlived its usefulness: Be quiet, respect authority, don't ask questions, and maintain the consensus. But in the late nineteenth and early twentieth centuries, during the so-called "Gilded Age," this kind of thinking made sense. To question authority in the coal mines or steel mills would mean unemployment and social stigma. For many unfortunate people who worked under slave-like conditions at that time, education was not a prized asset. The best one could do is work hard for his or her family, and be thankful to have any job, even if it was exploitive.

Unfortunately, however, this world view has been passed down, in most cases latently, from generation to generation without much interruption or reflection, even though the factories, mills, and mines are all gone. As the descendent of Polish, Welsh, and German descendents, I too was conditioned in my youth to believe in this nonsense. The coal is gone, replaced recently by natural gas, but the antiquated thinking remains the same. If politicians and the public really want change in the region, we need to start examining the thoughts that construct our reality.

~

In November 2010, I was asked to take part in a roundtable discussion for local radio and television. The topic was "Brain-drain in Northeastern Pennsylvania." Participating in the discussion allowed me to think more about my generation—those born after 1980—and our role in local events. In general, Pennsylvania has a high rate of college-educated young adults who leave the region upon graduating. The search for better jobs, more excitement, and a comfortable lifestyle lure many young adults to exit the region, thus leaving Northeastern Pennsylvania with a "brain deficit."

As I debated the topic with my fellow guests, I recalled when, two years before, I met Senator Bob Casey. A graduate student at the time, I was book browsing at a local Borders when I noticed the senator. Tall and unsuspecting, Casey was casually thumbing through a magazine when I approached him.

"Senator Casey?"

He turned and looked down.

"I apologize for interrupting you," I said, "but I just wanted to introduce myself."

I spoke with the senator for a few minutes, telling him about my career goals and plans after graduation. He seemed like a nice guy, and I was appreciative that he took time to talk. Finally, as our brief encounter came to an end, Casey made an unexpected, yet revealing comment.

"I hope you plan on staying in the area," he said. "We need smart young people like you to stick around."

Flattered by his compliment, I gave the only answer that I could at that moment.

"I'm not what I'm doing yet, but we'll see what happens."

Back at the television studio, I remembered Senator Casey's comment. It made me realize that *I* was a part of the very phenomenon that was being discussed. Many other twenty-somethings were leaving Northeastern Pennsylvania in hordes, and I—for reasons I still don't understand—was still here.

And for now, if I stay, I want to be a part of, and help shape, the larger conversation in an attempt to change the *status quo*. With corruption and dishonesty widespread, this is not the time to suspend our critical thinking faculties. Rather, it is the time to apply these faculties to the immediate people and events around us—which is the primary aim of this book. The people of Northeastern Pennsylvania have a critical choice about the future: Do we allow our social and political institutions to be run by fraudulent hucksters, fanatical demagogues, and faux experts, or do we seek a new understanding by applying new ways of thinking to the current state of affairs?

Eight Ways to De-Nepatize

1. Think about the issues that are important to you and how you can help bring about positive change. Don't just accept "That's the way it's always been," or "That's how we do things around here." Challenge the status quo.

2. Keep an open mind. Get information from a variety of sources, not only those that endorse your own point of view. If you listen to WILK, then try WFTE, the new local progessive station at 90.3 and 105.7 FM.

3. Engage in friendly debate with your family and friends. Don't be mean-spirited or obnoxious—encourage the exchange of ideas.

4. Get involved with local government. Attend school board and council meetings. Run for office yourself!

5. Find or start local grassroots groups to support. Volunteer your time or make a contribution.

6. Contact your local and state officials and representatives. Let them know your opinions.

7. Take advantage of technology. Read area newspapers and political blogs online. Find grassroots groups on meetup.com. Share information through social media.

8. VOTE! The old order in NEPA may finally be crumbling. We deserve something better!

Bibliography

American Civil Liberties Union of Pennsylvania, "Hazelton Residents Sue to Halt Harsh Anti-Immigration Law," *ACLU of Pennsylvania*, 15 August 2006.

Amerman, Kevin. "Sherwood a Charmer, Ore Recounts," *The Times Leader*, 8 August 2005.

Barrett, Duke. Interview by Kenny Luck, 25 April 2010.

Baumann, Michael. Interview by Kenny Luck, 16 December 2010.

Baumann, Nick, "Tom Marino's Free Pass," *Mother Jones*, 29 October 2010.

Betts, Heather. "Request for Interview with Bishop Martino," 20 April 2010, personal e-mail.

Billman, Jim. Interview by Kenny Luck, 10 April 2010.

Birkbeck, Matt, "DeNaples' Priest Had Deep Debt," *The Morning Call*, 4 January 2008.

Birkbeck, Matt, "GOP Congressman Candidate Thomas Marino Misreported Income," *The Morning Call*, 13 April 2010.

Birkbeck, Matt, "Rep. Carney: Show Me the Letter," *The Morning Call*, 1 September 2010.

Birkbeck, Matt, "Marino Changes Story," *The Morning Call*, 28 September 2010.

Birkbeck, Matt, "Marino Resigned While Under Review," *The Morning Call*, 1 October 2010.

Birkbeck, Matt and Christina Gostomski, "DeNaples' Priest Arrested," *The Morning Call*, 3 January 2008.

Brown, Stacy. "Legal Issues Complicate Rock 107 Host's Switch to WILK," *The Citizen's Voice*, 1 April 2010.

Cheek, Dan. Interview by Kenny Luck, 9 April 2010.

Chopyak, John A. "Bishop Martino is a Leader Who

Makes Necessary Change," *The Citizen's Voice*, 1 April 2008.

Corbett, Steve. Interview by Kenny Luck, 12 April 2010.

Corbett, Steve. "Yes We Can," WILK FM, 7 November 2008.

Couloumbis, Angela. "Judge Tells Defendants: Learn English 4 Spanish-speaking Hazleton Men Must Pass a Test to Avoid jail Time," *The Philadelphia Inquirer*, 28 March 2008.

Deabill, Eric, "Louis DeNaples Indicted," 30 January 2008.

Deakos, Dee. Interview by Kenny Luck, 5 May 2010.

Delazio, Sheena, "Ex-school Worker's Time in Fraud Case Likely 4–10 Months," *The Times Leader*, 30 December 2009.

Dewitt, Dick, interview by Kenny Luck, 6 March 2011

Ecenbarger, William. "In Pa. Coal Region, a Mother lode of Corruption," *The Philadelphia Inquirer*, 16 November 2009.

Ecenbarger, William. "Luzerne's Youth-Court Scandal, "How? Why?" *The Philadelphia Inquirer*, 25 October 2009.

Finnick, Renita. Interview by Kenny Luck, 8 April 2010.

Fox, Josh. Interview by Kenny Luck, 12 May 2010.

Gaia, Sarah. Interview by Kenny Luck, 10 May 2010.

Guydish, Mark, "The Damning Indictment of a Local Priest," *The Times Leader*, 2 January 2008.

Guydish, Mark. "Dunn Says He's Guilty of Bribe," *The Times Leader*, 17 December 2009.

Hall, Sarah Hofius. "Bishop Martino Rips College for Gay-Rights Speaker," *The Times-Tribune*, 17 February 2009.

Hall, Sarah Hofius. "Bishop Martino Says 'Tolerance' Has Limits," *The Times- Tribune*, 4 March 2009.

Hall, Sarah Hofius. "New Diocesan Leader Ends Bishop Martino's Stonewall of Teachers Union," *The Times-Tribune*, 14 October 2009.

Hamill, Sean D. "Mexican's Death Bares a Town's Ethnic Tension," *The New York Times*, 5 August 2008.

Hamilton, Maria. "The Constitutional Fight Over Holiday Symbols, and the So-Called 'War on Christmas,' *Find Law*, 24 December 2009.

Hazleton City Counsel, Official English Ordinance, 8 September 2006.

Henry, Sue. Interview by Kenny Luck, 27 May 2010.

Heydarpour, Roja. "Diocese of Scranton Mum on Sex Abuse Policy Case," *The Time-Tribune*, 13 July 2008.

Jackson, Peter, "Priest's Perjury Arrest Linked to PA Casino Probe," The Associated Press, 2 January 2008.

Janoski, Dave. "Kids-for-cash Scandal Draws Attention of Filmmaker Moore," *The Times-Tribune*, 26 April 2010.

Janoski, Dave and Michael Sisak, "This Time, for Keeps: Conahan Pleads Guilty to Single Count of Racketeering, Cannot Withdraw Plea If Unsatisfied with Sentence," *The Citizen's Voice*, 30 April 2010.

Janoski, Dave. "Game Plan," *The Citizen's Voice*, 12 May 2010.

Janoski, Dave. "The Sins of Our Fathers," *The Times Leader*, 9 July 2006.

Jones, Coulter. "Courthouse Pulls Nativity, Menorah Display to Avoid Lawsuit," *The Times-Tribune*, 18 December 2009.

Kick, Russ. *100 Things You're Not Supposed to Know.* New York: MJF Books, 2004, 241.

Kranish, Michael. "Pardons Reemerge as Issue in Clinton Run," *The Boston Globe*, 28 February 2007.

Krawczeniuk, Borys. "Local Clinton Backers, McCain Advisor Meet," *The Times-Tribune*, 20 August 2008.

Krawczeniuk, Borys, "Marino Contradicts in DeNaples Discussion," *The Times-Tribune*, 29 September 2010.

Krawczeniuk, Borys, "Marino: No More DeNaples Questions," The Times-Tribune, 19 October 2010

Krawczeniuk, Borys. "Results within Error Margins," *The Scranton Times-Tribune*, 7 November 2008.

Legere, Laura. "Bishop Takes Place on National Stage," *The Times-Tribune*, 30 November 2008.

Legere, Laura. "Parish Consolidations Through 2012 Will Leave Fewer Than 30 Across Lackawanna County", *The Times-Tribune*, 1 February 2009.

Legere, Laura. "Scranton Diocese Come Clean on Abusive Priest," 27 December 2008.

Lewis, Edward. "Ex-Pittston Area Board President to Face Sentencing," *The Times Leader*, 8 December 2010.

Lewis, Edward. "Murokski Involved In Crash," *The Times Leader*, 5 January 2010.

Lozano v. Hazelton, United States Federal District Court, 26 July 2007.

"Louis DeNaples and Mount Airy Casino Timeline," The Associated Press, 14 April 2009.

Lumia, Paul. Interview by Kenny Luck, 17 May 2010.

Lynn, Kevin. Interview by Kenny Luck, 28 April 2010.

Madonna, Terry G. Interview by Kenny Luck, 13 April 2010.

Marco, Kim. Interview by Kenny Luck, 16 May 2010.

Mauriello, Tracie, "Priest Accused of Lying about His Mob Ties in Casino Case," *Harrisburg Post-Gazette*, 3 January 2008.

Matza, Michael. "U.S. Appeals Court Hears Hazleton Case," *The Philadelphia Inquirer,* 31 October 2008.

Maslin, Paul. "Obama's Big Lead in the Polls is Real," Salon.com, 25 October 2008.

Mcauliffe, Josh, "The Rev. Joseph Sica Writes a New Book on Value of Forgiveness in Wake of Legal Troubles," *The Times-Tribune,* 8 December 2009.

McDonald, Joe, "Louis DeNaples' Attempt to Regain Bank Seat Thwarted," *The Times-Tribune,* 6 February 2010.

McDonald, Joe. "Cordaro, Munchak Indicted," *The Citizen's Voice,* 17 March 2010.

McDonald, Joe. "Cordaro, Munchak Arraigned," *The Citizen's Voice,* 19 March 2010.

McDonald, Joe and Sam Galski. "Appeals Court Upholds Judge Munley's Ruling on Hazelton's Crackdown on Illegal Immigration," *The Times-Tribune,* 10 September 2010.

McDonald, Joe. "Hate Crime: Guilty." *The Times-Tribune,* 15 October 2010.

McDonald, Joe. "Sexual Misconduct Allegations Surface against Former Scranton Jesuit," 1 December 2010.

McNulty, Evie Rafalko. Interview by Kenny Luck, 1 April 2010.

Morgan-Besecker, Terrie. "Piazza's Mail Fraud: 6 Months," *The Times Leader,* 1 April 2010.

Morgan-Besecker, Terrie. "Ex-PA Director Oliveri Sentenced," *The Times Leader,* 2 February 2010.

Morgan-Besecker, Terrie. "Intellacom Linked to Mail Fraud Charge," *The Times Leader,* 30 March 2010.

Morgan-Besecker, Terrie. "W-B Area Head Signs Plea Deal," *The Times Leader,* 3 February 2010.

Milbank, Dana "Homo Politicus: The Strange and Scary Tribes that Run Our Government," 2008.

Milz, Michael. Interview by Kenny Luck, 20 May 2010.

Moody, Erin. "Supporters and Detractors of Bishop Martino Having Their Say on Facebook", *The Citizen's Voice*, 2 April 2009.

Morgan-Besecker, Terrie. "Hazelton is Facing 2.4M Legal Bill," *The Times Leader*, 6 November 2010.

Ore v. Sherwood, Superior Court of the District of Columbia, 15 June 2005.

Oujdi, "Rumor: Obama's Internals in PA Apparently Leaked," Daily Kos, 14 October 2008.

Paige, Chris. Interview by Kenny Luck, 17 May 2010.

Paige, Chris. "Lou Barletta's Hazleton," 7 December 2009.

Pilchesky, Joe. "A Not-So-Proud History," *The Patriot News*, 15 November 2009.

Pilkington, Edward. "Jailed for a MySpace Parody, the Student Who Exposed America's Cash For Kids Scandal," *The Guardian*, 7 March 2009.

Powell, Michael and Michelle Garcia, "'They Must Leave', Mayor of Hazleton Says After Signing Tough New Law," The Washington Post, 22 August 2006.

Preston, Julia. "Judge Voids Ordinance on Illegal Immigrants," *The New York Times*, 7 July 2007.

Risch, Wayne. Interview by Kenny Luck, 10 April 2010.

Rubinkam, Michael. "Republican Congressman Paid Mistress Hush Money," The Associated Press. 4 November 2006.

Schetrum, Kim. Interview by Kenny Luck, 12 May 2010.

Schillinger, Charles and Steve McConnell, "For Lou

Barletta, Third Time's a Charm," *The Times-Tribune*, 3 November 2010.

Sica, Joseph, interview by Kenny Luck, 9 March 2010.

Sisak, Michael R. "Skrepenak to Resign amid 'Mistakes,'" *The Standard Speaker*, 17 December 2009.

Sisak, Michael R. and Dave Janoski, "Luzerne Commissioner Skrepenak Resigns and will Plead Gulity," *News Bank: America's Newspapers*, 18 December 2009.

Stark, George. Interview by Kenny Luck, 11 May 2010.

Staub, Andrew and Mia Light, "Kanjorski Falls," *The Citizen's Voice*, 3 November 2010.

Sullivan, Patrick. Interview by Kenny Luck, 3 May 2010.

Sweeney, Rory. "Media Inquiry," 14 May 2010, personal e-mail.

Swift, Robert. "Obama Strongly Carries Lackawanna, Luzerne," *The Citizen's Voice*, 5 November 2008.

Swift, Robert. "Severance Tax Dies," *The Citizen's Voice*, 22 October 2010.

Swift, Robert and Dave Janoski, "DeNaples, Sica Charges Dropped," *The Citizen's Voice*, 15 April 2009.

Tillman, Calvin. Interview by Kenny Luck, 11 May 2010.

The Associated Press. "Commissioners Remove Holiday Items from Luzerne County Courthouse Lawn," 17 December 2009.

Ungvarsky, Janine. "Indicted Pizzella Heads to W-B Area," *The Times Leader*, 8 December 2009.

Urbanski, Steve. "Corbett Calls Muroski Defenders 'Brainwashed' and 'Demented,'" *Scranton Public Policy Examiner*, 7 January 2010.

Urbina, Ian. "Despite Red Flags About Judges, A Kickback Scheme Flourished," *The New York Times*, 27 March 2009.

Vacula, Justin. Interview by Kenny Luck, 2 March 2010.

Wahner, Norman. Interview by Kenny Luck, 28 March 2010.

Winarski, Dawn. Interview by Kenny Luck, 10 May 2010.

Worden, Amy. "U.S. House Entices Hazelton Mayor," *The Philadelphia Inquirer*, 8 February 2008.

Electronic Sources

http://www.bishop-accountability.org/usccb/nature-andscope/dioceses/scrantonpa.htm

http://michaelbaumann.wordpress.com/

http://www.smalltowndefenders.com

http://blog.netesq.com/2006/07/illegal-immigration-and-crime-in.html

http://en.wikipedia.org/wiki/David_Duke

http://michaelbaumann.wordpress.com/2009/06/02/an-open-letter-to-bishop-martino-diocese-of-scranton/

http://www.usccb.org/nrb/johnjaystudy/incident2.pdf

http://www.wvwnews.net

http://www.pa2010.com/2009/12/lou-barlettas-hazleton

http://www.pamd.uscourts.gov/Lozano/decision.htm

http://www.huffingtonpost.com/2009/05/04/luis-ramirez-killers-foun_n_195535.html

http://www.economist.com/world/united-states/displaystory.cfm?story_id=15954262

http://www.epls.gov/epls/search.do?debar_recid=1682

&status=archive&vindex=0&xref=true

http://www.aclu.org/religion-belief/pennsylvania-county-agrees-remove-religious-symbols-courthouse-lawn

http://www.meetup.com/NEPA-Freethought

http://citizensvoice.com/news/courthouse-pulls-nativ-ity-menorah-displays-to-avoid-lawsuit-1.495916

http://www.pennlive.com/midstate/index.ssf/2009/12/holiday_items_removed_from_luz.html

http://www.aclu.org/religion-belief/pennsylvania-county-agrees-remove-religious-symbols-courthouse-lawn

http://www.writnews.findlaw.com/hamilton/20091224.html

http://www.985krz.com/pages/4753564.php#jeff

http://bigdanblogger.blogspot.com/2008/06/nepas-feminist-fraudster-wilks-steve.html

http://www.dailykos.com/storyon-ly/2008/10/15/05041/703/752/630799

http://www.salon.com/opinion/feature/2008/10/25/obamas_lead/

http://www.timesleader.com/news/Muroski-involved-in-car-crash-.html

http://www.wilknetwork.com/Saves-Lives--Don-t-Mourn-Lives/6106140

http://www.nytimes.com/2010/03/02/us/politics/02coffee.html

http://www.huffingtonpost.com/2009/04/15/gov-rick-perry-texas-coul_n_187490.html

http://www.nytimes.com/2010/03/02/us/politics/02coffee.html

http://thecatholicwatchdog.wordpress.

com/2008/02/21/a-message-from-bishop-martino/

http://www.religiondispatches.org/blog/human-rights/632/

http://www.democraticunderground.com/discuss/du-board.php?az=view_all&address=367x8041

http://thecatholicwatchdog.wordpress.com/2008/02/21/a-message-from-bishop-martino/

http://www.democraticunderground.com/discuss/du-board.php?az=view_all&address=367x804

http://gort42.blogspot.com/2006/04/radio-daze.html

http://en.wikipedia.org/wiki/Tony_Rodham

http://www.danamilbank.com/sherwood.html

http://www.youtube.com/watch?v=8D303Zo3nlk

http://www.msnbc.msn.com/id/35046453/ns/us_news-crime_and_courts/

http://citizensvoice.com/news/cabot-ban-inspires-county-partnership-1.732108

http://www.propublica.org/feature/frack-fluid-spill-in-dimock-contaminates-stream-killing-fish-921

http://www.nytimes.com/2009/11/03/opinion/03tue3.html

http://greenatheist.blogspot.com/2010/02/hate-mail-montage-from-december.html

http://www.slots.cd/pennsylvania-supreme-court-in-vestigation-01092008.html

http://www.educationforum.ipbhost.com/index.php?showtopic=17110

http://en/wikipedia.org/wiki/Louis_DeNaples

http://mafianewstoday.com/tag/louis-denaples

http://hosted.ap.org/dynaic/external/pre-election/bios

For information about bulk sales or to
arrange a personal appearance,
please email the author at
kennyluck@avventurapress.com

www.ingramcontent.com/pod-product-compliance
Lightning Source LLC
Chambersburg PA
CBHW021159010426
R18062100001B/R180621PG41931CBX00038B/69